Bread or Justice

Bread or Justice

**Grassroots Organizing in the
Welfare Rights Movement**

Lawrence Neil Bailis

Lexington Books

D.C. Heath and Company
Lexington, Massachusetts
Toronto   London

Library of Congress Cataloging in Publication Data

Bailis, Lawrence Neil
Bread or Justice:

Includes bibliographical references.

    1. Welfare Rights Movement—Massachusetts. 2. National Welfare
Rights Organization. I. Title.
HV98.M39 B3   322.4'4   73-15278
ISBN 0-669-91157-7

Published simultaneously in Canada.

Printed in the United States of America.

International Standard Book Number: 0-669-91157-7

Library of Congress Catalog Card Number: 73-15278

To my Parents

Contents

List of Figures

List of Tables

Foreword

The organization described in the pages that follow was part of a national movement of welfare recipients that emerged in the mid–1960s and spread rapidly from the big cities to smaller towns and rural counties. The movement began with small groups of AFDC mothers in different communities, each group acting disparately, with no knowledge of the others, but each acting on common and long felt grievances with "the Welfare" that had shaped and misshaped their lives. By June 1966 some of these groups had come together in a loose national affiliation and together they mounted a series of simultaneous demonstrations. The National Welfare Rights Organization takes this event as its birth date, for it marked the entry of the welfare rights movement into national public life.

The significance of that movement deserves emphasis. In 1966, when a startled New York welfare commissioner was confronted for the first time by a group of welfare recipients from the Lower East Side, he remarked that such a thing had not happened since the Depression. It is not hard to understand why this is so. Welfare recipients are very poor, and they share with most of the American poor the sense of unworthiness and powerlessness often labelled apathy. Sociologists are sometimes inclined to study these attitudes as if they were imbedded in a distinct lower-class culture which, mysteriously, perpetuates itself. More likely, the sense of unworthiness that the poor reveal has its sources in a larger American culture, that declares poverty to be shameful, a sign of failure, just as it declares wealth to be a sign of success. Similarly, the sense of powerlessness, of fatefulness, has its sources in an American political system that bars the poor from effective influence. But if the poor are ordinarily apathetic, and for good reason, welfare recipients are even more so, for they suffer not only the humiliations of the larger society, but the specific and systematized humiliations of the welfare system in which they are enmeshed and on which they depend for their barest survival. To be a welfare client means to be constantly reminded of one's unworthiness, and constantly reminded of one's powerlessness. And yet, in the 1960s, these people created a movement.

Of course, the welfare movement did not spring up full blown while all else was quiet. These were years of turmoil in the United States, particularly among blacks, and the larger black movement helped give welfare recipients the courage to make demands of the bureaucrats who ruled their lives.

The occasions of uprising by the very poor in the United States are infrequent, but they are not for that reason unimportant. The acquiescence of the most oppressed cannot always be taken for granted. Uprisings by poor and ordinary people, and the suppression of those uprisings by tactics ranging from electoral cooptation to armed military force, are very much part of the history of the United States. But it is the underbelly of history and has been given little attention by historians. Perhaps part of the reason for this neglect is that the struggles of common people are harder to study; their decisions, their battles, and their heroes are not marked down in the official records of events. They have to be reconstructed, pieced together from personal accounts, from occasional newspaper clippings, from court records and the like. But surely another part of the reason for the neglect is that historians are not persuaded that the history of poor people is as important as the history of presidents and generals and financiers.

Political scientists have shown a similar bias, and the political science literature is even more barren of accounts of collective action by the poor. But struggles by the poor, though often inchoate and shortlived, are nevertheless a part of the American political process. Indeed, the absence of such struggles much of the time is, as some observers have come to recognize, also part of the American political process, for it is a reflection of the way in which the American political system discourages political action by the poor and rebuffs such action when it occurs. When these movements surface despite these obstacles, they deserve study. They deserve the careful and close scrutiny that Larry Bailis has given the Massachusetts Welfare Rights Organization.

This book is not about the broad sweep of the black uprisings of the 1960s, or even of the national welfare rights movement. Instead, it is about the detailed inner workings of one state organization. While it is not less valuable for that reason, it does seem to me that a few words of caution are necessary, for Bailis' description of the internal mechanisms of the organization may disappoint some readers. We learn, for example, that welfare recipients were encouraged to join by the promise of material benefits, such as money for beds or a couch, and that their participation declined when there were no tangible gains to be made; that organizers stressed these material gains in dealing with recipients, and played down the militant tactics and the long-range goals of the national movement; and that decision-making in the organization was centralized. I think this account is accurate; these were all features of MWRO, and of local groups elsewhere in the country.

But that said, two points ought to be made. First, poor Americans are not nobler than other Americans; nor ought we expect them to be. To say that the welfare recipients who joined MWRO were moved to do so largely by the promise of material gain is merely to say that they acted like most other people do when they join unions or merchant associations or professional societies. What is different, and what made the Massachusetts effort so difficult, is that the poor people's organization depends for its continued vitality on the activity of its members, on their physical presence at meetings, demonstrations and the like. Most Americans may be joiners, but middle-class organizations require no such exertions from their roster of members, for they do not rely on the visible presence of large numbers of people to exert influence.

Similarly, to say that the Boston organizers were manipulative, or to say that decision-making was centralized in a small leader group, is also to point to commonalities between a poor people's organization and organizations that exist elsewhere in the social structure. And it ought to be added that there was in fact a rough democracy in these groups that went, I think, deeper than the formalities of democratic procedure, no matter what the organizers intended. Day by day, the organizers' success depended on their ability to enlist people, and their ability to enlist people, in turn, depended on their performance, on their ability to do the things their membership wanted. Few leaders of other organizations are as continuously on the line as these leaders were.

None of this is to argue that the "Boston model" described in these pages has been redeemed. The organizers were dedicated to building a permanent mass membership organization of the poor because they believed that organization meant political power. Measured by that goal, they failed. They failed for reasons which go beyond, I think, any weaknesses of the "Boston model," for reasons that have to do with the enormous obstacles to sustaining mass membership organizations among people who, even when organized, do not have sufficient power to win very much for very long. But before MWRO failed, it helped gain voice and force and money, if only temporarily, for the pariah class of success-ridden America, for people on relief.

What sort of goal is money? The welfare rights movement had a slogan, "Bread and Justice." For very poor people, a little bread is a little justice.

—Frances Fox Piven

Preface

It is not easy to prepare a scholarly analysis of the endeavors of a group of political activists whom one greatly admires, nor to write objectively about personal experiences in which emotions ran high. However, an author should reveal his potential biases to the reader as early as possible so that the reader can decide for himself whether any allowances should be made for subjectivity.

Therefore, I would like to state that I feel sympathy for the plight of welfare recipients, and anger that more has not been done for these Americans who lack the material means to meet their basic needs. It is probably impossible to remain neutral to a cause after spending over a year with individuals who are intensely dedicated to it; I do not pretend to have done so. The degree of involvement necessary to observe the inner dynamics of the Massachusetts Welfare Rights Organization has led me at times to think of the organization's members as "we" rather than "they."

At the same time, I have tried hard not to present an overly rosy picture of the MWRO history. Those of us committed to promoting social change have begun to realize that to expedite the discovery of paths to political effectiveness, efforts need to go beyond the random sharing of personal experiences by individual community organizers. One thing that is needed is a systematic analysis of the strengths and weaknesses inherent in the various strategies of leaders in the field. It is hoped that this review of the strengths and weaknesses of the welfare rights movement and of the Boston model of community organization will provide a step in that direction.

This study could not have been completed without the whole-hearted cooperation of the staff and lay leadership of the Massachusetts Welfare Rights Organization; their assistance and their patience with my questioning is deeply appreciated. Similar thanks is due to those officials of the Department of Health, Education and Welfare and the Massachusetts Welfare Department who consented to be interviewed.

Professor James Q. Wilson of Harvard University followed my research from its inception and provided assistance in the formulation of my ideas and the translation of those ideas into comprehensible English. Others who made helpful suggestions include Professors Nathan Glazer, Ralph Jones, and Lee Rainwater of Harvard University, and Professor Michael Lipsky of the Massachusetts Institute of Technology. Bill Pastreich and Tom Glynn of the MWRO staff reviewed the manuscript for accuracy and contributed many helpful insights as well. Hal Shear's contributions were twenty-fold.

Susan S. Bailis contributed to the completion of this volume in more ways than I can count—reacting to my ideas at such great length that I now find it impossible to distinguish my own contributions from hers, proofreading beyond the call of duty, and keeping my spirits up at those points when I despaired of ever finishing. Her help cannot be praised highly enough.

Bread or Justice

1 Introduction

Most efforts to persuade poor people that they could improve their living conditions by joining and participating in voluntary associations have met with limited success. More often than not, would-be organizers of the poor have returned empty-handed to report only apathy, resignation, and suspiciousness on the part of those they were trying to help. Some scholars have concluded that this result is inevitable, that the poor—or at least that segment of the poor they choose to label "lower class"—cannot be induced to participate in self-help or other political organizations at all. Edward Banfield, for example, puts it quite bluntly: "The lower-class person (as defined here) is incapable of being organized."[1]

On the other hand, much of the rationale for the community action programs and other elements of the "war on poverty" that emerged from the Economic Opportunity Act of 1964 depended upon the possibility of organizing poor people and conferring political influence upon them.[2] A review of the activities of Community Action Agencies, the civil rights movement, and the efforts of Cesar Chavez—to cite just a few examples—indicates that at least in some instances poor people have engaged in concerted activities that achieved some favorable results.

Not all participants in protest group activity in the past ten years have been poor; most antiwar demonstrations have been notably devoid of minority group participation. But the profusion of protest marches, sit-ins, freedom rides, boycotts, and above all, demonstrations suggests that we ought not question *whether* the poor can be organized to take concerted action but rather under what *conditions* this can be done. In particular, to what extent can poor people be organized into permanent lobbying organizations similar to those that new represent the interests of other groups?

In order to shed some light upon these questions, we have analyzed the most successful effort in this field to date—the activities of the welfare rights movement. The National Welfare Rights Organization (NWRO) has a membership that is undeniably poor—they are all welfare recipients. At its peak, it claimed from 75 to 125 thousand members throughout the United States.[3] In all probability it was the largest mass-based poor people's organization in the country.

The NWRO affiliate in Massachusetts is generally conceded to have been the most successful example of grassroots organizing within the welfare rights movement. Between June 1968 when the first NWRO organizer came to

1

Massachusetts and July 1970, more than 4000 women recipients of the Aid to
Families with Dependent Children (AFDC) public assistance program joined a
welfare rights organization in that state. In terms of its dues-paying membership,
the Massachusetts Welfare Rights Organization (MWRO) was second only to the
New York City welfare rights affiliate, a group that had nearly six times as many
welfare recipients from which to draw its membership. The June 30, 1969,
demonstration held by the MWRO on the Boston Common was the largest single
welfare rights demonstration in the country.

The procedures for building grassroots organizations, developed and refined
by the predominantly white, middle-class staff of the MWRO, were widely
studied and copied by welfare rights organizations throughout the United States.
These procedures, collectively known as "the Boston model," produced over 50
local affiliates for the MWRO in less than two years. (For a list of the sites of
MWRO affiliates, see Appendix A.) Each Boston model organizational drive
culminated in a demonstration at a welfare service office to demand "more
money now." Almost invariably, the demonstrators got what they were asking
for in the form of supplementary welfare checks for the purchase of food, clothing, furniture, or household supplies.

But despite these promising beginnings, only a handful of the MWRO local
affiliates were still active by the summer of 1970. Although some members
of the MWRO lay leadership continued meeting after this, there were no mass
actions involving the general membership after September 1970. At the present
time, the MWRO as herein described no longer existed. Although lay leaders
still represent the groups on various committees, all staff members have resigned
and many local groups are little more than "paper organizations"—a handful of
individuals helping each other out with individual grievances.

In this volume, we seek to shed light on both the potential for and limitations upon the efforts to organize poor people by carefully analyzing the initial
successes and subsequent inability to follow up on them by welfare rights organizers in the state of Massachusetts.

Both the rapid rise and the slow decline of the MWRO can be explained by
breaking the organization down into its principal components and observing the
different kinds of inducements to which each responded. The three major components of the welfare rights movement in Massachusetts were (1) the general
membership, consisting entirely of recipients of public assistance; (2) the elected
lay leadership, also welfare recipients; and (3) the MWRO staff who were non-
recipient organizers. (The terms organizer and staff member are used interchange-
ably.) Each of these three components looked at the welfare rights movement as
a means for fulfilling different needs. The MWRO organizers hoped to build pressure groups of poor people. The general membership was relatively uninterested
in building pressure groups but responded to promises of tangible benefits that
organizers promised in return for coming to the first meeting and demonstration.
As some members became lay leaders, a third point of view developed: these

leaders began looking beyond the tangible material benefits toward maintaining themselves in office and hence maintaining a position of prominence and respect in their own communities and in the larger society. It should be noted that none of the three was deeply concerned with reforming the welfare system.

The genius of the Boston model was in structuring organizing drives and early local affiliate activities so that they met the diverse needs of all three groups. Because of a relatively obscure (until that point) "loophole" in the public assistance regulations in Massachusetts, MWRO organizers were able to promise welfare recipients that if they participated in welfare rights activities, they would soon be rewarded by supplementary welfare grants totalling hundreds of dollars. By making the receipt of these benefits contingent upon joining a local welfare rights organization and participating in its activities, the organizers were able to induce large numbers of welfare recipients to attend meetings and demonstrations. The organizers needed members to have a group, the leaders needed members in order to lead, and the members needed the group to get their benefits (or so they thought).

With the passage of time, however, these motivations could no longer be coordinated, and both the MWRO statewide organization and its local, affiliated welfare rights organizations began to founder. Because of the positive feedback that invariably followed a Boston model organizing drive, the MWRO staff confined its efforts almost exclusively to the planning and execution of additional drives rather than attempting to address the more troublesome questions of how to maintain membership interest in existing groups. The lay leadership generally opposed organizational expansion, in part because it might lead to the development of challengers to their incumbency. In addition, the more sophisticated lay leaders began to perceive that they could continue to receive recognition as leaders even if they failed to continue the dreary tasks necessary to maintain interest on the part of their membership. Many of the general membership gained enough confidence to make demands of the welfare office personnel without belonging to a group; others soon found that after a few major supplementary welfare checks had been won, there was little more that the group could continue to offer them.

Thus all components in the welfare rights movement—members, organizers, and leaders—began to lose interest in maintaining the local affiliates, and the groups began to fade away. The failure of the MWRO was its inability to build upon the foundation laid by the Boston model with a program that could maintain the need fulfillment of members, organizers, and leaders. The problems faced by the MWRO in transcending the Boston model were not mere accidents of any circumstances in Massachusetts in the late 1960s but instead represent major problems that any effort at community organizing among the poor must recognize and ultimately overcome. It is therefore hoped that this review of the MWRO experience will prove useful to all community organizers and students of social policy.

A note on objectivity: the information presented in this volume was derived primarily from fourteen months of full-time, participant observation of the activities of the Massachusetts Welfare Rights Organization. During this time, the author not only performed clerical work in the MWRO statewide office but provided transportation for staff, leaders, and members to attend various meetings, rallies, and demonstrations. This direct observation of the MWRO was supplemented by assembling a clipping file on welfare rights activities and by collecting printed materials and records of the welfare rights movement in Massachusetts and elsewhere. Interviews of varying degrees of formality were completed with public welfare officials in Washington, D.C., and Boston and with welfare rights organizers and leaders from various parts of the country, while more structured interviews were conducted with the MWRO staff and a leadership sample of recipients.

It should be recognized that this research design, leaning so heavily on personal conversation and participant observation, may lessen objectivity. Contact with MWRO staff members was more frequent and open than with the lay leaders and members of the organization, and it is possible that a bias towards the staff point of view on basic issues of community organizing—especially in terms of organizer-lay leader disputes—will be evident despite efforts to remain impartial. In like manner, contacts with Welfare Department personnel occurred with far less frequency but greater formality than with either MWRO staff or leaders and thus another bias may have been introduced.

A note on terminology: in this volume, individuals are generally described as either "poor people" or "middle class." This usage obviously lacks rigor, but rather than become embroiled in such controversial issues as the incidence and exact nature of a "culture of poverty,"[4] reliance has been placed on a simple dichotomy.

The key to the success of the welfare rights movement has been the provision of benefits that can be obtained almost immediately. Poor people who have remained indifferent to past organizing efforts promising rewards in the vague future have responded to welfare rights recruiters offering tangible benefits receivable in a week or two. But it is difficult to say whether they have done so because they have developed short "time horizons" and an inability to postpone gratification (and thus are "culturally lower class") or because, being poor they could not afford to gamble time, resources, and effort for something that may happen some time in the future (and thus are "situationally lower class.") Without extensive in-depth interviewing to determine the perceptions and attitudes of poor people and without a longitudinal study observing poor people both before and after they have been approached by organizers, it is virtually impossible to distinguish between the case in which a culturally lower-class individual has been induced to join an organization and one in which a situationally lower-class individual has done the same thing.

Millions of Americans lack the resources to live at a standard above the

poverty level, lack influence in community decision-making, and have no immediate prospect of changing these conditions. (This last qualification eliminates
the temporary or voluntary poor, such as students.) These Americans, who
have generally not participated in voluntary self-help organizations, are herein
labelled "poor." Everyone else is labelled "middle class," the term being used
as a substitute for "non-poor."

2 Historical Context

Probably no beneficiaries of a public subsidy have less real influence on the terms and conditions of that subsidy than do the recipients of public assistance. . . . Only one group of assistance recipients speaks through its own leaders, the National Federation of the Blind. . . . There is no comparable mechanism for ferreting out the views of deserted or widowed mothers as to the adequacy of the ADC programs, its impact on the beneficiary, and grass roots suggestions for change in that category. . . . But it is certainly not impossible that the groups themselves can be organized and led by a compassionate clergyman or other outsider.

—Gilbert Steiner[1]

The year 1966 was marked by the birth of a movement that made Steiner's words outdated almost as soon as they were written. In the early months of that year delegates from poor people's organizations from all parts of the country met in Syracuse, New York, and Chicago, Illinois, to discuss the need for unity among grassroots organizations.[2]

At this same time, Richard Cloward and Frances Fox Piven of the Columbia University School of Social Work, were circulating the draft of an article that was later to appear in *The Nation* as "The Weight of the Poor: A Strategy to End Poverty."[3] The thesis of the article was that widespread dissemination of information about eligibility for welfare benefits could vastly increase the welfare rolls and hence create a bureaucratic and fiscal crisis, which in turn would lead to the replacement of the existing public assistance programs with a guaranteed annual income. Cloward and Piven were most concerned with selling this thesis to fledgling community groups than with receiving academic criticism; their efforts did come to serve as a link between such groups.

The sequence of events that led directly to the founding of the NWRO began in May 1966. At that time, Dr. George Wiley, a former Associate Director of the Congress of Racial Equality (CORE), and two of his former associates in that organization set up a mimeograph machine in a two-story row house in Washington, D.C., and christened the building the Poverty Rights Action Center (PRAC). It was Wiley's initial intention to create PRAC as a permanent headquarters for coordinating the efforts of existing poor people's organizations.

The first project undertaken by PRAC was the planning of a nationwide series of demonstrations to be coordinated with an already planned welfare

7

recipients march from Cleveland to Columbus, Ohio. The idea for this march had been conveyed to the Ohio welfare recipients by representatives of Cesar Chavez's United Farmworkers Organizing Committee at the Syracuse meeting referred to above.

As a result of the efforts of PRAC, "poverty rights" demonstrations involving (reportedly) thousands of participants in 16 major cities took place on June 30, 1966. The demonstrations in New York, Washington, Chicago, Los Angeles, Baltimore, and Boston, among other places, received extensive coverage in major newspapers.

Although the NWRO has since referred to the June 30 demonstrations as "the birth of a movement," there was at that time no formal tie between the participating groups. The activities in each city were sponsored by broad coalitions of groups—not only by welfare recipient organizations. With the passage of time, however, coordination and cooperation between the welfare recipient groups that had demonstrated on June 30 gradually increased, and eventually a nationwide recipients organization was created.

In August 1966 representatives of welfare recipient groups from 24 cities met in Chicago and voted to form a "National Coordinating Committee of Welfare Rights Groups," the NCC. A December meeting of the NCC formally designated the PRAC Office as headquarters for a welfare rights movement. In February 1967, the NCC authorized PRAC to devise a uniform membership card for all affiliated groups. Two months later, the NCC adopted uniform membership requirements and a common dues structure for its affiliates.

The culmination of all these steps came in August 1967. Delegates from 67 local welfare rights organizations met in Washington, D.C., and formed the National Welfare Rights Organization by adopting a constitution that had been drafted by the PRAC staff and adopted by the NCC. The latter preserved a role for itself in the new organization as the principal decision-making body in the national structure. But despite the creation of a nationwide organization, the local welfare rights groups retained almost complete autonomy for local activities.

During these early months of the welfare rights movement, two major decisions were made that were to play a crucial role in determining the nature of its grassroots organizing activity. The first of these was a narrowing of focus from seeking to create a movement for all poor people to concentrating on recipients of public assistance. The focus upon welfare recipients was, for the most part, unplanned. In the words of a veteran NWRO organizer, "the welfare recipient groups just grew so quickly that they soon took up everyone's time." The new movement concentrated its energies on those targets where its measurable performance was by far the greatest—on the easily organizable welfare recipients. As was later the case with the organizing strategies of the Boston model, the problems of the NWRO in seeking a broader constituency resulted from its dwelling on the great successes in a single, narrow segment of its original goals.

The second decision was a rejection by Wiley and his followers of the Cloward-Piven strategy of flooding the welfare rolls with new recipients in favor of one based on the organization of current welfare recipients into pressure groups. In part, this decision, like the first, was based on the relative ease of organizing current welfare recipients by offering them tangible benefits in the form of supplementary welfare payments. Not only was it more difficult to identify people who were *eligible* for welfare than those who were already *recipients*, it was also more difficult to motivate the former to act.

NWRO critics of Cloward and Piven have argued that it is easier to create a welfare crisis than to affect its resolution. Without political power, say these critics, activists would be reduced to a strategy of "create a crisis and then pray." Despite this rejection of their advice, Cloward and Piven have remained close friends and advisors to Wiley and his successors and have sometimes jokingly referred to themselves as the "loyal opposition." In particular, they have continued to criticize grassroots organizing—according to the Boston model—as both excessively costly and diverting of organizers' time away from more fruitful endeavors.[a]

The first major lobbying activity of the newly formed NWRO was directed against the work incentive provisions of the Social Security Amendments of 1967. The NWRO demonstrations, including a sit-in in the Senate Finance Committee hearing room, brought the new organization much publicity but apparently failed to have a significant impact in the shaping of legislation.

The year 1968 brought the welfare rights movement a number of important victories. In the spring of that year, the NWRO won major concessions from the Rev. Martin Luther King, Jr., which gave welfare rights leaders and issues an important role in the Poor People's Campaign. This success in capitalizing on

---

[a]Although the "flooding the welfare rolls" strategy was first presented in 1966, Cloward and Piven still believe it to be the most appropriate. They feel that the vast expansion of the welfare rolls since 1966 has not led to an adequately funded guaranteed annual income proposal because there has not been *enough* of a crisis rather than because of any gaps in their theory. The authors' *Regulating the Poor* published in 1971 elaborates on the theme first presented in *The Nation*:

"The NWRO's contribution to the welfare explosion would have been greater had it devoted fewer resources to organizing existing recipients and placed more emphasis on mobilizing the non-welfare poor to get on the rolls. The NWRO, however, has generally considered it more important to build up its membership rolls than to build up the welfare rolls (on the dubious premise that poor people can develop political power through permanent membership organizations.)"[4]

The evidence presented in this volume suggests that the history of the welfare rights movement has neither entirely confirmed nor denied the validity of the Cloward-Piven criticisms of the Boston model strategies of community organizing. As will be shown in Chapter 4, the two writers' doubts about the ability of the MWRO affiliates to maintain themselves over long periods of time were borne out. But at the same time, the welfare rights movement did gain exposure and perhaps influence on the national level.

the Poor People's Campaign was a major factor in promoting the first meeting
between the NWRO leadership and a Secretary of Health, Education and Welfare,
which took place in the summer of 1968.[b]

NWRO reached another major milestone in December 1968, when it was
granted a sizeable government contract to help monitor the Work Incentive
Program (WIN), which constituted the major innovation of the very same 1967
Social Security Amendments NWRO had so bitterly opposed the year before.
This funding and several large foundation grants helped finance major expansion
of the NWRO staff to include field organizers.

Armed with growing membership rolls and increased prominence in the
mass media, NWRO won greater success to government officials during the first
Nixon administration. Welfare rights leaders were among the first to meet with
Daniel P. Moynihan after his appointment to the White House staff and began
meeting regularly with Secretary Robert Finch of the Department of Health,
Education and Welfare and his top assistants. NWRO leaders were consulted by
the Nixon administration in the drafting of the Family Assistance Plan and were
active in lobbying against it.

Despite continued demonstrations directed at Congress and the Department
of Health, Education and Welfare—including a take-over of Secretary Finch's
office—as well as more traditional lobbying and negotiating efforts, it is largely
misleading to speak about welfare rights activities at the national level. Rather
than relying on such centralized activity, the welfare rights movement has typically relied on simultaneous demonstrations, based on common themes, by local
affiliates throughout the country. NWRO publications and press releases have
been dominated by accounts of the activities and accomplishments of its local
affiliates, examples of which include the original series of rallies on June 30,
1966, as well as the "birthday in the streets" demonstrations each succeeding
June 30. Nationwide coordinated campaigns have revolved around the demand
for supplemental welfare checks to pay for back-to-school clothing for the
children of welfare recipients and the demand for retail credit for NWRO members at major department stores.

At the August 1969 NWRO Convention in Detroit, Michigan, speakers and
press releases referred to a movement with between 30,000 and 100,000 members. Internal documents upon which delegate strength at that convention was

---

[b]Throughout its history, the NWRO has shown a remarkable facility for capitalizing on
events planned or sponsored by others. The original June 30, 1966, demonstrations were
planned in part by welfare rights activists attending a meeting called by an ad hoc committee for a guaranteed annual income. NWRO meetings have often been scheduled to
coincide with conventions of social welfare voluntary associations, at which the welfare
rights leaders have been invited guests, in order to provide further economies and "troops"
for demonstrations. The rump session of the December 1969 White House Conference
on Food and Nutrition, which was planned in part by welfare rights staff and which
endorsed the NWRO demand for a guaranteed "adequate" income of $5500, is probably
the most successful use of this tactic to date.

based revealed a total of roughly 22,000 dues paying members. Higher public claims are justified by movement leaders who note that each dues-paying member is the head of a family that probably averages three or four members and thus about 25,000 families could be calculated to contain at least 75,000 individuals. More than two-thirds of these paid memberships were concentrated in 9 major industrial states. The states with the largest membership were, in descending order, New York, California, Pennsylvania, Michigan, Virginia, Massachusetts, Ohio, New Jersey, and Illinois. When broken down by cities, New York City had by far the largest membership; there were more members in Brooklyn than in any other city in the country. Boston groups had the second largest total membership, while Detroit, Los Angeles, and Chicago completed the list of the top five cities.

The Welfare Rights Movement
in Massachusetts

The history of welfare rights organizing in Massachusetts antedates the creation of the MRWO by several years. The original banner around which welfare recipients in that state were organized was that of the Roxbury (Boston) based Mothers for Adequate Welfare (MAW).[5]

Boston was one of the first target cities for the Students for a Democratic Society (SDS) community organizing efforts under the Economic Research and Action Project (ERAP) adopted in December 1963. The organizations—such as MAW—that eventually emerged from the ERAP efforts greatly reflected the SDS biases against hierarchy and in favor of participatory democracy. For years after its founding in the summer of 1965, MAW functioned without formal membership requirements or by-laws, without regularly scheduled meetings, and without elected officers.

MAW's most noteworthy mass action was a sit-in by 30 members in a Boston welfare office in June 1967. The police action to clear the building of demonstrators was followed by three days of "disturbances"—described by some as riots—in Boston, a fact that has never been forgotten by all those faced with demonstrations led by MAW's successors in the MWRO.

MAW was visited in the spring of 1966 by Richard Cloward and its members later took part in the June 30, 1966, demonstrations coordinated by the PRAC. MAW representatives went to the early meetings of the National Coordinating Committee of Welfare Groups, but they became disenchanted by the increasingly prominent role played by non-recipient organizers on the staff of PRAC. MAW representatives did however take part in the August 1967 convention at which the NWRO was formally organized.

In June 1968, George Wiley used private foundation funds to hire Bill Pastreich—an Alinsky-trained community organizer—and sent him to Boston to help build new local chapters of MAW. It is still debated whether the (lay) leadership of MAW had asked Wiley for assistance or whether he had sent Pastreich on his own initiative. Whatever the case, Pastreich arrived with the understanding that he was to stay for a three-month trial period, after which he could remain only if asked to do so by a vote of the welfare recipient lay leadership. MAW leaders did eventually demand that Wiley remove Pastreich from the State, but by that time, Pastreich had been able to build more than a half dozen local groups that were loyal enough to him to demand that he stay.

MAW began to fade from public view shortly after the denunciation of Pastreich, and the Pastreich-led groups soon monopolized all welfare rights activity in the state. It was these Pastreich-led groups that banded together in October 1968 to form the MWRO, the primary focus of this study.[6]

Bill Pastreich had developed an early version of the Boston model before he ever set foot in Massachusetts. After a few weeks of making preliminary contacts and recruiting part-time assistance from a diverse group of individuals, he began organizing drives in 5 separate locations but gave most of his personal attention to a public housing project in the Roxbury section of Boston. In August 1968, the 5 new groups began a series of coordinated demonstrations at their local welfare offices. Each demanded supplementary welfare checks for the purchase of furniture and household supplies. In addition, they pressed for the establishment of precise standards or "guidelines" that spelled out exactly those items of furniture to which every welfare recipient was entitled and how much could be spent on each.

Pastreich's concentration upon the single site paid off as the bulk of the media and hence public attention centered on the Roxbury group and the welfare office in which it was holding a sit-in. An initial capitulation by harried Welfare Department officials led to the granting of almost all the individual requests of the Roxbury demonstrators. This event—known as "the bonanza" in the folklore of the MWRO and as "Black Tuesday" by some disgruntled state legislatures—led to increased pressure by the other groups for similar rewards and also helped recruit additional members for the Roxbury group.

By the end of the month, the Welfare Department had agreed to the promulgation of furniture guidelines. Although the guidelines were not as generous as the welfare rights leaders might have wished for, they were perhaps the best in the country, and the August demonstrations were correctly viewed as major successes by welfare recipients throughout the state. Even more importantly, the promulgation of guidelines meant that Pastreich had achieved the major organizing tool that he needed for future recruitment drives based on the Boston model.[7]

These successes and their prominent coverage in the media created a climate that Pastreich was quick to exploit in gaining new members for his original 5 groups and in seeking to organize new ones. His growing reputation made it easier for him to recruit and train a more-or-less full-time organizing staff and thus reduce his reliance on clergy and other part-time help.

Pastreich and his followers quickly organized four additional groups in the metropolitan Boston area and in October 1968 brought representatives of the 9 welfare rights organizations together to create a formal statewide structure. The first meeting of the Massachusetts Welfare Rights Organization, as the new state-wide group was called, was held in the Roxbury headquarters of the local group that had scored the initial breakthrough. The initial statewide leadership elected at that time was dominated by leaders from the Roxbury group, and except for two brief interludes, this domination continued throughout the history of the organization.

The Boston model was further refined as the MWRO organizing staff grew more proficient in applying it. New groups were organized on almost an assem-bly line basis. The basic issue in each drive was the demand for special needs grants, usually selected from the list of items on the state-approved furniture guidelines. Another demand was for "food orders"—supplementary checks for members to buy turkeys at Thanksgiving and Christmas. Perhaps the least suc-cessful MWRO activity during this period was a sit-in for special needs payments for winter clothing. Held in the Massachusetts State House, this activity brought the new organization its first arrests and considerable publicity but little in the way of tangible gains.

In the winter of 1968–69, the statewide leadership of the MWRO approved a set of by-laws drafted with the assistance of MWRO staff members. These by-laws provided for an annual membership convention at which statewide officers would be elected and major policy decisions made. The first of these annual conventions was held in February of 1969. By that time, the MWRO had grown to include 16 local groups.

The spring and early summer of 1969 witnessed not only the beginning of MWRO campaigns to win credit at retail stores and to gain special needs grants for Easter clothing but also the increasingly professionalized organizing drives built around the demand for furniture and household supplies. A June 30, 1969, MWRO rally to celebrate the third birthday of the welfare rights move-ment drew several hundred welfare recipients and ten or fifteen times as many non-members of the organization to the Boston Common. The choice of Dr. Benjamin Spock as major speaker ensured wide coverage by the national media. Many feel that this was the largest welfare rights rally anywhere in the nation.

The arrival of summer meant increased availability of students and recent college graduates for full-time organizing. MWRO staff meetings that could once be accommodated in Pastreich's small apartment living room were now attended by 30 to 40 people jammed into the portion of the MWRO storefront statewide headquarters set aside for large gatherings. By the end of the summer, 12 additional organizing drives had increased the total MWRO membership by over 50 percent. The MWRO delegation to the NWRO national convention in August 1969 was credited with representing over 3000 members in 32 local groups.

The MWRO full-time staff declined in size as the 1969–70 school year began, but was augmented by some students who worked part-time and by other new recruits. As the staff and lay leadership grew in experience, they began to question the value of continually "grinding out" new groups at the expense of devoting time and attention to the problems of strengthening existing local affiliates. Although this issue was raised with increasing frequency, it was repeatedly pushed into the background by the pressing need to make decisions about ongoing organizing drives or planned statewide demonstrations.

There was a MWRO speaker at the Moratorium Day rally on the Boston Common on October 15, 1969, but the major antiwar activity of the group took place the day before—this date being chosen to capitalize on press interest in the Moratorium without risking burial of the story among the hundreds of other events that would take place on Moratorium Day itself. The theme of the demonstration was a "shop-in" at the Boston Army Base's post exchange to dramatize the fact that federal money was going to the military establishment and not towards feeding the poor. Roughly 100 members of the MWRO responded to the efforts of their organizers to insure a respectable turnout at the army base.

A stiffening of Welfare Department responses to MWRO demonstrations in the fall of 1969 cast doubt about the "numbers equals power" theory of the Boston model. A major demonstration in Springfield, Massachusetts, involving hundreds of welfare mothers failed to bring capitulation on the demands for winter clothing despite the support of a considerable number of students and widespread civil disturbances prompted by it.

The organizing momentum of the previous summer continued into the fall and winter in large part because of the desires of the staff to hone their organizing techniques as close to perfection as possible. By the end of 1969, 13 more local welfare rights organizations had been created, which raised the total MWRO membership to over 4000.

By the last months in 1969, the MWRO was approaching a crucial period in its development that involved several major transitions: Many organizers began looking for ways to transcend the Boston model; Pastreich had decided he would soon be leaving and thus created the problem of finding a replacement; and the second annual MWRO convention, scheduled for February 1970, created the problem of succession of lay leadership. In addition, the Massachusetts governor announced a "welfare reform" plan that eliminated special needs payments.

If the organization had successfully weathered these challenges, it would have been well on its way towards institutionalization. But none of the transitions went smoothly. In the spring of 1970, considerable thought was given to the development of new models that would unite welfare recipients and other poor people in common activities, but none were ever implemented under welfare rights auspices. Pastreich's successor as chief MWRO organizer was never able to win the total confidence of the staff; staff resentment finally led to his resignation several months later. (The staff then discovered that it was no easier to replace Pastreich's successor than it had been to replace Pastreich himself.)

The February 1970 lay leadership elections created an even greater crisis and for the remainder of the year, the MWRO devoted almost all of its energies to internal matters. As the February convention and election drew near, the incumbent lay leadership sought to postpone the convention and to extend their term of office by one year. By firmly resisting this plan, the staff created deep conflict with the leaders. In his last major decision before leaving the organization, Pastreich led the fight against the postponement by telling the MWRO lay leaders: "You can try to do this, but I'll fight you with everything I've got, every step of the way."

The convention took place as scheduled in February 1970, but the MWRO was thrown into chaos by the defeat of most of the incumbents, including the statewide chairman from the original Roxbury group who lost to the leader of a newly organized Roxbury affiliate. The defeated leaders refused to accept the results. Claiming that fraud had taken place, they joined with other community groups, including the Black Panthers and remnants of the MAW organization, to attack the new leaders as "lackeys" of the white, middle-class organizing staff. (This was the first time that the race of the staff members had ever played a significant role in MWRO affairs.)

Adding to the problems faced by the MWRO at this time was a December 1969 announcement by the state's governor of a major "welfare reform" that would eliminate the special needs grants provisions of the welfare law, upon which the Boston model was dependent, in favor of a "flat grant system." Faced by a potential body blow to the organization, the MWRO leaders and staff both remained pessimistic about the prospects of reversing the governor's decision and continued devoting the bulk of their attention to internal matters.

By the spring of 1970, increased hostility between organizers and lay leaders, as well as the resignation (for personal reasons) of a number of local group organizers, led to a reduction in the number of local welfare rights affiliates that had the services of full-time or half-time organizers. As the links of local groups to the statewide organization weakened, fewer and fewer of them took part in coordinated or statewide activities. Without the impetus provided by the staff, many local groups ceased functioning entirely. MWRO activity during this period was largely limited to those 10 or 12 groups that still had organizers or whose lay leadership retained close personal ties to members of the MWRO staff.

A large proportion of MWRO attempts to "show the flag" at this time were carried out by a handful of people. MWRO staff and loyal lay leaders met with officials of social welfare organizations in Massachusetts such as the National Association of Social Workers in order to plan a common lobbying strategy against the proposed "flat grant" welfare reforms. A few MWRO leaders testified against the flat grant proposals at legislative and other public hearings. (The defeated faction felt so strongly about the flat grant that they testified at some of the same hearings but gave no public indication of the MWRO's internal crisis.) At times, the new MWRO leaders were able to assemble a few dozen members to carry out such activities as an attack on the Welfare Department's computer installation, a sit-in in a radio station, and harrassment of a number of speeches by the governor. These efforts captured enough publicity so that many observers of welfare rights activity did not suspect that anything was amiss for months.

By July 1970, the internal crises of the MWRO had reached a temporary resolution. Plans were being made for new organizing models, and Pastreich's successor had been replaced by a transitional staff director who held the confidence of the remaining staff members. The lay leadership struggle ended with the resignation of the newly elected statewide chairman and several of her followers who were replaced by the original leaders they had defeated in February. But the organization was never able to recover the lost momentum and again attain the prominence of its first year and a half of existence. Little by little the MWRO organizers drifted away and left an active lay leadership but little grass roots strength.

The Formal Structure of the Welfare
Rights Movement

Although there have been variations in detail, the formal structure of the welfare rights movement has remained constant since the creation of the NWRO in August 1967. Each element of that movement has been organized according to the same model—a staff serving at the pleasure of a board of elected lay leaders who retain final responsibility for the determination of basic policy. The lay leaders of a local welfare rights affiliate have the power to fire their organizer whenever they feel he is not serving their interests, and statewide and citywide leaders can hire or dismiss their staff directors as they please. Thus, George Wiley could serve as executive director of the MWRO only as long as he retained the confidence of the national leaders of the movement. (As is often the case in voluntary associations, this formal description does not accurately portray the actual distribution of influence. The welfare rights staff have exercised far more influence than might be assumed on the basis of this description alone.)

Local Level

Officially, each local affiliate of the NWRO is autonomous:

> Each local welfare rights group is fully independent. It decides on
> its own program, makes its own decisions, organizes itself, raises its own
> money. . . . The NWRO National Headquarters serve as a resource and
> communications [sic] for local welfare rights groups. The NWRO
> Executive Committee and the National Coordinating Committee develop
> and recommend nationwide campaigns.[8]

Although there have been efforts at persuasion by NWRO staff members, local
welfare rights organizations have often ignored them.

The only major power that NWRO holds over its local groups is the power to
recognize them as affiliates. According to the original NWRO constitution, in
order to be so recognized, a local group must have at least 25 members who have
paid one dollar annual dues to the movement's national headquarters in Washington, D.C. The constitution also requires that these members include a majority of welfare recipients and that all but 10 percent be low-income persons. In
addition to this, each local group must be independent of any larger organization that could restrict its freedom of action.

The official program of the August 1969 NWRO Convention claimed over
300 local affiliates. but an internal document prepared to calculate delegate
strength at that convention contained, quite surprisingly, a higher figure.
According to that document, there were 523 local welfare rights groups throughout the United States, 376 of which had the required 25 or more dues-paying
members.[9] Although many of them were short-lived, the MWRO alone organized over 50 local welfare rights affiliates in the first two years of its existence.

Elected lay leaders form local group executive boards and have final say on
all activities for their membership. Although they do not often have the
resources to recruit their own organizers, they do have the power to dismiss
them.

Intermediate Level

In many places, local welfare rights organizations have banded together in
regional groupings, either on a citywide level as in New York City or Chicago
or on a statewide level as in Massachusetts or Connecticut. (In some areas both
citywide and statewide organizations can be found but usually at least one of
them exists only on paper.) NWRO has not promulgated any regulations for
affiliated intermediate level organizations across the country. The following
description therefore refers to the intermediate level organization that existed
in Massachusetts.

The key to the formal structure of the MWRO was the annual convention
that was open to all members of affiliated local groups. The primary function of
these conventions was the election of officers for the MWRO statewide executive board and of representatives to the national level National Coordinating

Committee (NCC). The annual conventions were supplemented by monthly meetings of delegates of affiliated groups that served to disseminate information about welfare rights activities throughout the state and to adopt or modify policy proposals put forward by the MWRO executive board. The statewide executive board met weekly and served as the principal decision-making body in the MWRO.

Just as the MWRO executive board had complete freedom to ignore any suggestions from the national level of leadership, local groups had the similar option of ignoring the directives of the statewide executive board. These options were often exercised.

The MWRO was more closely knit than many intermediate level welfare rights organizations because of its highly structured organizing staff. Organizers from the local groups and the central office staff met together at least twice a week to plan activities, compare notes, and arrive at common positions to present to the lay leaders.

National Level

The key structures on the national level of the welfare rights movement are the direct analogues of those in the MWRO: members elect lay leaders who have the power to dismiss the staff director. A biennial convention of delegates from all local groups in the country elects a national executive board. The National Coordinating Committee (NCC) consists of delegates from each state that contains a local welfare rights affiliate, and meets four times a year to make basic policy decisions for the NWRO. The national staff of the NWRO is responsible to the national executive board in the person of the executive director, formerly, George Wiley and now Johnie Tillmon, a former welfare recipient.

The NWRO executive board has always been representative of the largest states within the movement—that is, those that have been entitled to the greatest numbers of delegates at the national conventions. At the 1969 national convention, one of the leaders of the MWRO was elected to the NWRO executive board in recognition of that state's growing power within the movement. The 1971 national convention symbolically ratified the decline of the MWRO by failing to choose any major officer from Massachusetts.

3 "Boston Model" for Grassroots Organizing

The Boston model, as conceived by Bill Pastreich and implemented by the MWRO, was in many ways a cookbook for community organizers—it contained a detailed set of instructions to guide the neophyte's every step. The model was simple enough to be quickly assimilated and implemented by would-be organizers with no previous experience yet reliable enough to virtually guarantee a successful demonstration if all its instructions were faithfully followed. Pastreich and his followers conducted over 50 organizing drives based on this model within a two year span and in so doing were able to enroll over 4000 welfare recipients as dues-paying members for the MWRO. Although no detailed document explaining both the underlying principles of the Boston model and the nuances of its implementation has ever been produced, there was enough of a consensus to allow an observer to do so.[a]

The most important premise of the Boston model was that abstract slogans could not be relied upon to elicit a positive response among large numbers of welfare recipients. Instead, this could only be done by making believable promises to bring about changes that would have a direct, tangible impact upon people's lives. Promises, in turn, could be made believable only by delivering on them quickly. From these insights, one can derive the first fundamental principle behind the Boston model—and for the most part behind most welfare rights organizing throughout the country:

1. The typical welfare recipient will make the sacrifices of time, energy, and resources to join a self-help or lobbying organization if, and only if, she is convinced that doing so will bring her tangible benefits that are quickly realizable.

Although the slogan "bread and justice" has been a battlecry of the welfare rights movement, the battle for justice has failed to motivate most welfare recipients; all they want is more bread. The welfare rights movement was successful in providing that bread because of the unique provisions of public assistance

---

[a]A six-page mimeographed paper entitled "The Boston model" was drawn up by Pastreich and Rhoda Linton, a welfare rights organizer from New York City. This paper, together with samples of MWRO leaflets, has been widely circulated within the welfare rights movement as an aid to training. The term "Boston model" in this study, however, refers to all the activities employed by MWRO staff in organizing drives for which the mimeographed paper serves only as a bare outline.

regulations that have generally allowed supplemental welfare benefits in times of "special need." Had it not been for this "cooperation" by the government in providing the bread, the insight behind the Boston model would have been intellectually interesting but useless in practice.

In addition to describing a procedure by which tangible benefits could be won, the Boston model also included a number of steps designed to neutralize attitudes held by many poor people that have often frustrated community organizing efforts. Perhaps the most crucial of these psychological barriers has been apathy and resignation—particularly the absence of a belief that anything positive could emerge from one's own efforts. Charles Silberman describes the problem as one in which "slum residents will not stir unless they see some reasonable chance of winning, unless there is some evidence that they can change things for the better."[1]

For many of those contacted by welfare rights organizers, resignation was accompanied by a fear that making harsh demands for supplementary benefits would alienate the welfare caseworkers who had been so kind to them in the past.

Suspicion of outsiders who claim to want to help has been a second major barrier to building a poor people's organization. The would-be community organizer who is not generally known in a neighborhood must first convince people that he is sincerely committed to providing help and is not just another exploiter. He must prove that he is willing to make a substantial commitment to those who join with him, that he will not merely leave within a month or two if the fancy strikes him, and, furthermore, that he is not an "outside agitator," a radical, a Communist, or perhaps even a hippie.

A third barrier has arisen from the rejection of militance and violence most poor people apparently share with the majority of the American public. In particular, welfare rights organizations, such as MWRO, have had to overcome a reputation for toughness created by such activities as those of the original Roxbury group that had won the Massachusetts furniture guidelines. Anyone hoping to recruit members thus had to overcome the organization's mass-media image that stressed boisterous demonstrations and conveyed the threat of arrests.

A negative attitude towards public assistance and the status of welfare recipients has created a fourth barrier in that many poor people, including those contacted by the MWRO, are unwilling to identify themselves publicly as welfare recipients. Unless this attitude were modified, it would have been impossible to recruit them for a protest-oriented recipients' group.

The combined impact of these attitudes—as well as the general lack of experience with formal voluntary associations on the part of most welfare recipients—made it virtually impossible for the welfare poor to form large scale lobbying organizations on their own despite the existence of tangible rewards they could accrue in doing so. The burden of building such

organizations therefore lay upon outsiders who could so structure people's out-
looks that they saw the benefits of organization as outweighing the sacrifices.

This is no easy task. The Boston model provided for dealing with the
problem through direct person-to-person persuasive efforts that began with a
door-to-door recruitment program and continued throughout the entire time
the recruited individual was affiliated with the organization. From this, one
can derive the second fundamental principle of MWRO organizing:

> 2. The promise of tangible benefits can be made credible and the
> negative attitudes of poor people towards community organization
> overcome only with intensive and continuing personal contact
> between MWRO organizers and the general membership.

Implementing this principle meant that the Boston model required a fairly
sizeable non-recipient organizing staff that ideally included one full-time
organizer for each local affiliate and many more to take part in the organizing
drives. The MWRO—and the entire welfare rights movement—was aided
immeasurably by sympathetic private foundations and by the federally funded
antipoverty programs whose contributions provided a large proportion of the
payrolls required to support staffs large enough for organizers to devote personal
attention to individual members.

But even with direct personal attention and the provision of tangible benefits, there were still limits to the loyalty that could be developed among welfare
recipients. This limitation thus forced the introduction of a third fundamental
principle:

> 3. Because of the great difficulties in motivating poor people to
> participate in organizational activities, demands made on the mem-
> bership should be minimized: the less asked, the better.

Much of the success of the Boston model in gaining the participation of large
numbers of poor people was the direct result of its ingenuity in defining the
required participation almost entirely in terms of performing those tasks that
were necessary in order to receive supplementary welfare benefits.

Aside from paying the nominal NWRO dues of one dollar per year and any
dues that the local group might have established, all that the welfare rights
organization asked of its membership was that they demand benefits in an
organized way. In order to receive supplementary benefits, a welfare recipient
must normally make a direct request of his caseworker, who then fills out the
necessary forms. By distributing supplementary grant request forms in meeting
halls during the speech-making and election-of-officers proceedings, the MWRO
staff was able to create a sense of purpose for the meetings for those who might
not have attended without such direct personal motivation. Furthermore,

bringing those who have filled out the forms to the welfare office in groups, the staff brought about at least the appearance of organized group protest activity. Regardless of how the individual members viewed their actions, the rest of the world perceived that a demonstration had taken place.

As will be discussed in a later chapter, difficulties in organizational maintenance arose when the staff tried to make further demands upon the membership—for example, to take part in a demonstration or meeting that did not have any immediate connection with the receipt of benefits. But until that point, things generally ran smoothly.

The Boston model was thus built around three perceived necessities: the need to offer tangible benefits, the need for personal contact in order to overcome negative attitudes, and the need to minimize the demands upon the membership. A series of pragmatic assumptions spelled out the best way to meet these necessities and thus determined the standard operating procedures of Boston model organizers. The first of these propositions dealt directly with the problem of demonstrating the usefulness of the group to potential members:

> The best way to convince poor people that an organization can bring them tangible rewards is by winning them quickly, and by carefully associating the benefits with organizational activity.

This proposition rules out strategies that involved the membership in time-consuming preparations for the initial demonstration. The ideal strategy from this point of view would have been to provide the benefits as soon as someone joined. The existence of provisions in the welfare regulations, which permitted supplementary grants in times of special need and the assignment of discretion to disburse these benefits at the lowest levels in the Welfare Department, made the local welfare offices the most obvious source of the needed benefits. The key to winning these benefits and thus assuring the future growth of the local welfare rights organization was a clear-cut and well-publicized victory in the welfare offices.

During demonstrations within welfare offices, the primary goal of the MWRO staff was to demonstrate as clearly as possible that it was collective action of the group that was winning the benefits. Wherever possible, negotiations with Welfare Department personnel were to be carried out in front of the assembled membership, not behind closed doors with just a delegation of recipients. Similarly, whenever anyone was able to win a benefit, she was urged to share her experiences with everyone else in the group.

The second proposition concerned the way in which this initial victory at the welfare office could be achieved:

> The chances of victory—especially when making a new demand— are directly proportional to the size of the crowd gathered at the welfare office.

Normally benefits had to be won through on-the-spot bargaining during the demonstration. The larger the crowd of recipients in the office, the greater the disruption—or more precisely the potential disruption—and hence the greater the bargaining power of the leaders of the demonstration, provided that the protest group leaders could assure Welfare Department personnel that they could control the crowd.

It might be argued, following a line of reasoning suggested by the writings of Thomas Schelling, that the bargaining power of the protest group leadership would have been even greater if they could not guarantee the future behavior of the crowd saying that "If you do not capitulate quickly and grant our demands, there is no telling what will happen." To a certain extent, this tactic was employed. But it was a dangerous one for those seeking to build a permanent organization. If the first demonstration got out of hand, arrests might have followed. Arrests, in turn, would have further fed the fears and suspicions of the potential members and the future development of the welfare rights group would have been thrown into doubt.

Simply put, the Boston model called for the mobilization of as many people as possible in order to strengthen its own legitimacy as well as the motivation of the local Welfare Department staff to get the group out of the office as quickly as possible.

A third subsidiary proposition flowed from the requirement that the leadership be able to commit themselves to getting the group out of the office once the initial demands were met. This would only be possible if the general membership understood why they were in the welfare office and if they were willing to accept orders from their leaders:

> The best way to ensure that those taking part in the confrontation
> at the welfare office understand what is going on and are responsive to
> the requests of the leaders of the demonstration is to hold a meeting
> directly before the confrontation at which the organization is fully
> explained and the confrontation leadership is elected.

The second and third propositions led directly to a fourth:

> In order to maximize the number of knowledgeable participants
> in the welfare office confrontation, one needs to maximize the
> number of participants in the preceding meeting.

This chain of reasoning can, in turn, be carried still further backwards, addressing the problems of attracting a large crowd to the initial meeting and of preparing them for the upcoming confrontation. The answer to both of these problems was derived from the second fundamental principle:

> The best way to get people to the first meeting is through direct

face-to-face discussion with the potential members. This permits an
attempt to link the purposes of the group with whatever personal
problems are facing the individual recipient at the time.

The suspicion of outsiders referred to earlier presented a dilemma to would-
be organizers. In order to deal with this, the Boston model provided for a
"team approach" to recruiting:

> In face-to-face meetings with potential members, fellow welfare
> recipients are more likely to receive a warm welcome than are college
> student, middle-class organizers. But recruitiers who are welfare recip-
> ients are less likely to understand the dynamics of building a welfare
> rights organization and would be less likely to deliver the required
> recruiting "pitch." Therefore, a team consisting of a welfare recip-
> ient (hopefully from the same neighborhood) and an organizer would
> be the ideal organizational recruiters.

Personalized contact by organizers and fellow recipients with the prospective members provided the vital link between the goals of "more money now"
and the specific pieces of furniture that each recipient felt she needed. Personalized contact also helped insure a smoothly run first meeting and thus a
further increment of control during the first confrontation. A campaign based
on leaflets mailed to recipients and posted in prominent areas *might* have overcome the apathy of significant numbers of poor people and draw them to a
meeting at which tangible benefits were to be distributed. But in order to build
a continuing organization, a large measure of spadework had to be done to prepare members for that meeting. At minimum, each individual had to know that
he was going to participate in the birth of an organization that would in turn
be the source of his benefits. If the idea of forming an organization were presented at the first meeting without any advance warning, many recipients
might have become confused; others might have felt tricked or misled. Beyond
this, the unpredictable nature of a large meeting of welfare recipients could have
hampered attempts at explanation of the new group and its objectives. The
idea of forming a group to win benefits was this assumed to be more easily
absorbed when it was first presented on a face-to-face basis and thus heard for
a second time at the meeting.

The MWRO achieved this personalized contact by visiting recipients in
their own homes, in what were known as "doorknocking campaigns." The
final subsidiary proposition in the Boston model addressed the prerequisites
for a successful doorknocking campaign:

> The efficiency of a recruitment drive will generally be increased if
> a list of names and addresses of current welfare recipients can be
> obtained, and other preliminary planning completed as well.

In public housing projects, there was often a high enough concentration of welfare recipients to justify knocking on every door in each building. More often, however, a procedure of going from door-to-door in a neighborhood would have been a waste of time and manpower because most of those contacted would not have been welfare recipients and hence would have been eligible for the tangible benefits promised at the first meeting. Thus an initial investment of time in obtaining or preparing a list of recipients in the area was considered well worth the trouble. In addition to assembling lists of recipients, MWRO organizers also spent much of the preliminary planning time in deciding such questions as how big an area should the drive cover, what issues should be stressed in the campaign, and when would be the best time to begin.

Reviewing this series of propositions and transposing it into chronological order, we see that the process of building a welfare rights group, according to the Boston model, can be divided into four distinct steps:

1. Planning and preliminary decisions.
2. "Doorknocking"—the first contact with potential members.
3. The first meeting.
4. The first confrontation (and the first victory).

The successful completion of each step laid the foundation for the next. The successful completion of the last step meant that the drive had met its basic objective, a new local welfare rights organization had been born. The remainder of this chapter will consist of a detailed description and analysis of each of these steps as they occurred in a typical Boston model organizing drive.

Planning and Preliminary Decisions

As soon as a decision was made to build a new local welfare rights organization in Pilgrim City,[b] the MWRO staff director delegated all responsibility for day-to-day decisions about the drive to a single organizer, called the drive organizer, and assigned several recent recruits to the staff to work under him. (Bill Pastreich played the role of drive organizer himself during the first months of welfare rights activity in Massachusetts, but as soon as he had trained his subordinates sufficiently, he delegated his authority to them.) From moment of assignment until the completion of the first confrontation, the drive organizer,

---

[b]There is no such place as Pilgrim City in Massachusetts. The name has been chosen to represent a neighborhood of a large city such as Boston or an entire smaller city or town. In like manner, references to the "Pilgrim City Welfare Rights Organization (PCWRO)" should be construed as indicating an "ideal type"—a typical welfare rights organization organized according to the Boston model.

who was expected to consult with Pastreich and other members of the staff, held the entire responsibility for all decisions and their execution.

One of the first decisions to be made was determining the boundaries of the target area that was to be organized. This decision—like all others—was made almost entirely in terms of a single criterion: maximizing the chances of a successful first confrontation at the welfare office. Given the proposition that the chances of victory are proportional to the number of recipients crowded into the welfare office, boundaries were drawn so that everyone in the target area went to the same welfare office; the principle of minimum demand eliminated the possibility of asking some members of the group to attend demonstrations in other people's welfare offices.

The drive organizer faced two competing criteria in choosing the size of the target area. Maximizing turnout suggested as large a target area as possible, but minimum demand required that members live close to the welfare office. If the welfare office was more than a short distance from the hall in which welfare rights meetings were held, or the meeting hall too far from the members' homes, large numbers of members would participate only if transportation were provided. Hiring buses would put a severe strain on the limited resources of the MWRO and was thus avoided wherever possible.

If the welfare office were at a great difference from most recipients in an area, the demand to open a satellite or branch office might be an excellent organizing issue. Unfortunately, however, this demand could not be met with alacrity and an early response was vital in terms of future growth of the group. One local welfare rights group in Massachusetts failed and others have run into difficulty on these grounds.

The issues of race and ethnicity also became involved in the drawing of boundaries for the target area, and again conflicting criteria were introduced. Maximum turnout suggested that blacks and whites as well as English-speakers and Spanish-speakers should be combined into a single group. Both the MWRO general membership and organizers have shown a preference for integrated organizations stressing the common bonds of poverty and not race. On the other hand, meetings at which all announcements need to be translated into Spanish or Portuguese and then back again tend to become boring, and the problem of controlling a bi-lingual group during a demonstration becomes exacerbated. In Pilgrim City, the combination of segregated housing problems and the need to organize in compact neighborhood areas led to the decision to establish several groups, each one dominated by a single racial or ethnic group.

The decisions concerning the choice of issues and the timing of the drive were closely intertwined. Certain issues, such as supplementary grants for back to school clothing, provided natural focal points for organizing drives during the appropriate months of the year. Others such as supplementary grants for furniture could be used any time.

The Boston model required that all issues chosen for a drive meet three requirements. They all had to (1) relate to pressing needs of welfare recipients with (2) some tangible assistance (3) in the immediate future. Many idiosyncratic problems facing welfare recipients, such as failure to receive one's check on the day it is due, meet all three requirements and could conceivably form the basis for welfare rights recruiting campaigns.

Such campaigns have in fact been the basic pattern in a number of areas, perhaps most notably in Brooklyn, New York. In Brooklyn, welfare rights recruitment was based on a model calling for the presence of welfare rights staff or experienced members in welfare offices at all times in order to provide assistance to anyone coming to that office with a complaint. Assistance was provided only for those who agreed to join a local group. On occasion, groups would wait until a significant number of individual grievances had accumulated and then threaten a mass sit-in until everyone's complaint was satisfactorily settled. This pattern of recruitment does not fit into the framework of what we have called a drive since it can be carried out continuously.

The Boston model rejected this idea in favor of organizing drives based on common demands such as the demand for supplementary welfare checks to meet unusual circumstances. Wherever state law has provided for these special needs grants, it has been proven more efficient to build organizing drives around them because all members can be convinced that they have a common need at the same time; otherwise, an organizer must wait until a recipient develops a complaint. The idiosyncratic model was employed in Brooklyn primarily because the New York welfare laws no longer contained provisions for special needs grants.

In choosing an issue, the primary criterion used by the Pilgrim City drive organizer was (apparent) legitimacy. The issue would have to appear legitimate to the recipient (since she must be convinced that she can gain the benefit) and to the Welfare Department officials (since the group needs a victory at the first confrontation). The key to establishing legitimacy was precedent—that is, being able to demonstrate that some individual had already received special needs grants for a given purpose in the past. In the words of one MWRO organizer, "It's all a question of precedents: to find 'em, to make 'em, or to fake 'em."

Bill Pastreich's first major goals in Massachusetts were to establish precedents for distribution of supplementary grants for furniture and then to force the state to issue guidelines that spelled out precisely which items of furniture and household supplies all recipients were entitled to own. With these initial victories accomplished, the MWRO had an excellent organizing tool, and the Pilgrim City drive organizer chose to take advantage of it. The Pilgrim City drive was based on furniture needs; the basic message presented to each recipient was the same:

> *Do each of your children have their own bed? Did you know that*
> *you are entitled to a separate bed for each? Come to the first meeting*

*of the Pilgrim City Welfare Rights Organization. At that time, we'll
fill out individual request forms based on these provisions of the law
and then we'll turn them in at the welfare office. In no time at all,
you'll have the furniture.*

Relying on easily winnable issues creates the danger that recipients would be
encouraged to go to the welfare office on their own and make their demands
privately. The Boston model dealt with this problem by providing only generali-
ties about eligibility for special needs benefits during the initial contacts with
recipients and stressing the group's monopoly over the request forms. These
forms were available only to members and only at group meetings. If someone
chose to attend a meeting, join the group, fill out the forms, and then take them
to the welfare office on her own, there was little that could be done about it.
But this was not often the case since the recipient had already joined the welfare
rights group and perceived of it as the source of the forms that enabled her to
gain the benefits. MWRO organizers emphasized their role by placing the name
of the local group prominently on all request and appeals forms.

In other states, welfare rights groups went even further in developing a monopoly of benefits for their membership; for example, the provisions of Michigan
law providing for supplementary benefits for special diets for those with malnutrition were seized upon by welfare rights groups who developed request forms
and provided doctors to certify to the malnutrition of all their members. Similarly, welfare rights groups in New York reportedly provided both forms and
referrals to podiatrists for members to get special grants for new shoes.

Conceivably, a welfare department could have destroyed this monopoly
by instructing caseworkers to inform all recipients of all benefits to which
they were entitled and by distributing its own request forms. But given the
budgetary constraints on welfare departments as well as the growing public
annoyance with rising welfare expenditures, this action was never undertaken
nor does it appear likely that it ever will.

In the MWRO, the use of special needs grants as an organizing tool was
refined close to its ultimate potential. Negotiations between the organization's
leadership and the Massachusetts Welfare Department resulted in guidelines
that provided a state-sanctioned minimum furniture standard; recipients were
generally considered entitled to any item of furniture on the approved list
merely by proving that he did not currently own it. The MWRO staff prepared
thousands of copies of this list which formed the basis of most of its organizing
drives. (A copy of this form is in Appendix B). According to the Boston model,
potential members were allowed to look at the lists and asked which items they
did not own. Whatever items they lacked would be granted to them—if they
joined the organization (or so they were told). Because no welfare recipient in
Massachusetts was likely to have every item on the minimum standards list,
promises of furniture and household appliances were virtually guaranteed to
draw the interest of most potential members.

An even more powerful use of special needs grants would have been the addition of the threat that "if you don't get it now, you'll never get it" to the organizing pitch that promised tangible goods in the immediate future. The opportunity to conduct such a campaign occurred twice in Massachusetts—once when the state legislature passed a welfare reform measure that apparently put an end to the practice of giving special needs grants for furniture except in cases of natural disaster, and again when the Governor provided for the end of virtually all special needs grants by introducing a "flat grant" system.

In the first case, the MWRO scheduled a major organizing drive in the heart of Boston to climax shortly before this furniture "freeze" went into effect. Despite the fact that most MWRO organizers were disappointed with technical aspects of the drive, it drew several hundred recipients—the most ever—to the first meeting. (An intensive lobbying campaign following the passage of the legislation resulted in administrative rulings that negated the intent of the legislation. But neither the MWRO staff nor those whom they organized could have been sure of this in advance.)

By the time the Governor's flat grant proposals came into effect—at the end of the summer of 1970—the MWRO had deteriorated to the point where no major drives were mounted to take advantage of the occasion. This proves that it takes more than an ideal issue or opportunity to mount a successful drive; at minimum, it takes a skilled staff of organizers, which the MWRO was losing at an accelerating pace at that time.

The timing of the Pilgrim City organizing drive dictated that no seasonally available supplementary grant could be used. Since the choice of furniture as an organizing tool left a good deal of leeway as to the exact date at which the first meeting would take place, other factors became important. In this case, the first meeting and first confrontation of the Pilgrim City Welfare Rights Organization were planned to coincide with a series of planned demonstrations by other welfare rights affiliates throughout the state. Since first meetings were invariably better attended than subsequent meetings of the same groups, the plan to coordinate the first meeting of new groups with demonstrations of others helped swell the total number of recipients demonstrating on a given day. By releasing the total figures to the press, the MWRO was able to add to its reputation as a powerful statewide organization. In addition, coordination of the Pilgrim City meeting with other demonstrations enabled the Pilgrim City organizer to reassure the more hesitant members of this group that. . .

> *within an hour or two more than 20 other groups throughout the state will be going to their welfare offices and making similar demands. This really proves the power that comes from poor people working together.*

Questions of race and ethnicity affected the timing of welfare rights

organizing drives as well as the boundaries of target areas. Many poor whites
have seen the black welfare recipients as more militant and perhaps less worthy
than they. Since there were two adjacent neighborhoods to be organized in
Pilgrim City—one white and the other black—the drive organizer decided to run
the drive in the white one first. Had he done it the other way, the publicity
from a militant demonstration by a black welfare rights group might have dis-
suaded many of the whites from later assembling under the same banner.

Because so many things could go wrong, the drive organizer held off any
direct recruiting activities until he felt sure that all necessary groundwork had
been laid. At minimum, this meant that an adequate number of MWRO staff
was available to help with the doorknocking, that the area had been surveyed
for potential friends and enemies, and that a list of names and addresses of
welfare recipients in the area had been assembled.

As soon as he had been appointed, the drive organizer began making contacts in Pilgrim City. Given the initial suspicions of the recipients, his job
would have been impossible if well-respected community leaders had spread
doubts about the strangers that had come into the area. Once the local group
was on its feet, it would have the strength to disregard its detractors, but until
its first meeting, first confrontation, and first distribution of tangible benefits
to its members, the Pilgrim City WRO was vulnerable. Therefore, if the formal
and informal neighborhood leaders passed the word that welfare rights organization was worthwhile, the job of the organizers was simplified.

Although the Pilgrim City organizer made persistent efforts to win the
sympathy of a few community leaders, he did not attempt to recruit any of
them for leadership roles in his new group.

Many community leaders were not welfare recipients and were thus ineli-
gible to join, but even when they were recipients, their status as established
leaders made them unlikely candidates for the day-to-day work of community
organizing, which involves spending long hours knocking on recipients' doors.
Established leaders were also considered to be more difficult to "educate" and
hence more likely to reject the advice of any newcomers such as the MWRO
staff.

During this preliminary phase of the drive, the drive organizer gave special
attention to Pilgrim City's antipoverty agencies and its churches. In other
drives, the antipoverty agencies had been a major source of resources, manpower,
and even meeting places. In this case, the organizer was able to convince the
director of the Pilgrim City Community Action Program to permit agency staff
to use their typewriters, mimeograph machines, and stationery to prepare flyers
that would be sent to people on the agency's mailing lists as well as those
suggested by the drive organizer. The flyers were then mailed with the agency
postage meter. Although the Pilgrim City CAP director had agreed to all of this,
he refused to assign any of his clerical workers or neighborhood aides to help the
drive organizer as one or two of his counterparts in other cities had done.

Sympathetic CAP staff members, however, were helpful in revealing grievances held by welfare recipients in the area and in suggesting recipients who might be persuaded to help out with the doorknocking. The agency continued to be a major contributor of the PCWRO once it had gotten on its feet by providing direct cash grants to hire buses for welfare recipients to attend mass rallies and for "training sessions"—the MWRO staff was always quite liberal in defining training whenever proposals were submitted to the CAP director.

The support of religious leaders was also valuable in the organizing drive, especially in dispelling the suspicions and hostility to the outsiders who had entered the Pilgrim City community. Although the MWRO staff had at times been able to recruit priests, nuns, or ministers to join the doorknocking teams, in this case, support from the clergy was limited to a letter of endorsement for the drive, written by a well-respected local priest and mailed on church stationery. Had he failed to get this letter, the drive organizer would have used the following general letter:

> *The Human Rights Commission of the Archdiocese of Boston endorses the organizing of welfare recipients being carried on by the MWRO, affiliated with the NWRO. It is our opinion that it is to the benefit of everyone in Massachusetts, and poor people in particular, that this work succeed. We recommend participation with and in this organization.*

These letters were mailed out in advance and carried by organizing teams; they proved useful in gaining a positive reaction during first contacts with potential members.

The Pilgrim City priest also gave permission to use his church for the first meeting and for local group offices, in the hope that if this were done potential members would be less likely to perceive the group as "radical." The presence of the priest at the first meeting and his delivery of the opening prayer provided the first salvo in a carefully orchestrated progression of speeches to convince the new members to proceed to the welfare office after the meeting for the first confrontation:

> *Oh Lord, bless these people as they set out to gain what is rightfully theirs. May their first meeting with Mr. Welfare Director be a successful one . . .*

The Pilgrim City drive organizer turned for support to the management of the local public housing project. The manager offered to convert an empty apartment into a permanent local group office and to provide a basement room for local group meetings. This offer enabled the organizer to choose an office and meeting room that met the principle of minimal demand, although he chose the church for the first meeting for the reasons outlined above. While storefront offices and meeting rooms might also have met the principle of minimum demand, they were ruled out in this case—as in most—because of their inordinate costs.

The process of scouting the neighborhood for potential friends and enemies remained largely an art even in Massachusetts because it was impossible for any organizing model to provide detailed instructions about how to proceed in this phase of the campaign. The acquisition of a list of names and addresses of all welfare recipients in the neighborhood was, on the other hand, one of the most important and most fully developed aspects of the Boston model. Possession of such a list was considered so important that it was almost a sufficient reason to plan a drive in a given neighborhood. Had the Pilgrim City drive organizer been unable to obtain a list, he would almost certainly have cancelled the drive.

Not only did a list permit doorknockers to concentrate all their energies on potential members, but it also permitted an initial mailing to prepare welfare recipients for their first contact with the doorknockers. In keeping with the principles outlined above, the Pilgrim City drive organizer put together a packet of materials for the initial mailing in an effort to link membership in the PCWRO with the receipt of tangible benefits and to allay potential members' suspicions with letters of endorsement from the priest and from a few welfare recipients in the area who had consented to serve as an "organizing committee." Dissemination of the packet just before the doorknockers began their work increased the curiosity (and desire for benefits) of potential members and this proved helpful in getting the doorknockers into people's homes.

The most complete and up-to-date lists of names and addresses of welfare recipients are in the files of the local welfare office. Unfortunately—for drive organizers—most welfare administrators do not release these lists to welfare rights staff on the grounds that such actions would violate federally mandated confidentiality provisions. The legal authority for this refusal is ambiguous, as federal legislation and regulations have wavered first in one direction and then the other throughout the history of the public assistance program. In general, it is now agreed that states cannot reveal names and addresses of recipients if this information would be used for either "commercial or political" purposes. MWRO staff generally did not press for such public disclosure due to membership disapproval of such a tactic.

Although the most direct route for the acquisition of the lists—asking for them—was unuseable, the Boston model provided organizers with a number of alternative procedures. Wherever possible, MWRO organizers sought to find sympathetic caseworkers who might be induced to "loan" their records overnight so that copies could be made. Partial lists of recipients were also sought from the CAP agency's records of programs that catered heavily to welfare recipients. The drive organizer also checked to see whether any local businesses kept separate records for customers who made purchases with Welfare Department vouchers in order to "borrow" those records.

Although several partial lists were obtained by these methods, the Pilgrim City drive organizer tried to supplement them by setting up a recruiting table at a place where local recipients were known to congregate. To do this, he relied on the regularity introduced into the lives of welfare recipients by the twice-monthly arrival of their basic welfare checks. On each of these days—known to recipients as "check day"—most recipients made an effort to be home to meet the mailman and then proceeded almost immediately to cash the check. By discovering where recipients cashed their checks, the drive organizer easily calculated where and when he could meet the optimum number of potential members in the shortest time.

The "check day" cycle also played an important role in the future activities of MWRO affiliates as well. Whether an event took place just before or just after check day greatly affected its chances of success. Dues were collected, for example, shortly after check day, when most recipients still had a good deal of money. Sensitivity to such nuances was a major factor in the MWRO ability to build poor people's organizations.

In Pilgrim City, most recipients cashed their checks at a supermarket, although in other localities banks or other business concerns were favored. The drive organizer asked to set up a recruiting table adjacent to the check-cashing window, but when this request was refused, he settled for permission to place a table directly beside the main entrance.

After the table was set up, recipients had to be induced to pause and engage in conversation. This was accomplished in part by having a member of an existing welfare rights affiliate man the table and confront each passerby with the direct question "Are you on welfare?" Other MWRO lay leaders, circulating through the store, asked this question to likely looking people and then directed them to the table. Flashy posters with catchy phrases were also used in the hope that they would strike the fancy of potential members. *"Do you have enough?"* asked one of the posters. The drive organizer's knowledge of the area and its local grievances enabled him to set up other posters in the form of a simplified roadside Burma shave promotion:

DO YOU HAVE ENOUGH SHEETS AND PILLOW CASES?
WELFARE RIGHTS MEMBERS GET ENOUGH SHEETS AND
PILLOW CASES.
ORGANIZE AND GET WHAT YOU NEED.

Each person who approached the table was given a flyer explaining that welfare rights members win tangible benefits and disclosing the time and place of the first meeting of the Pilgrim City Welfare Rights Organization. Those manning the table spent some time answering questions, but for the most part, they concentrated on getting names and addresses and then promised that everyone would be personally visited in the near future at which time further questions would be answered. Along with the initial mailing, meeting recipients at the recruiting table served to ease the acceptance of the doorknockers when they first appeared.

In addition to facilitating the preparation of lists of names and addresses, the table served several other useful purposes as well. The most promising women who came to the table were asked to attend special meetings to learn about the organization and then serve on the doorknocking teams. The table also helped attract publicity through the press, radio, and television, which not only aided the organizing drive but also helped build public recognition for the group that was to prove useful in future lobbying campaigns.

Using all these techniques, the drive organizer accumulated a list of several hundred welfare recipients in Pilgrim City. Since everyone on this list had to be visited personally for fifteen or twenty minutes, the drive organizer soon realized that he needed a sizeable team of assistants before beginning the door-knocking campaign to contact recipients in time for the first meeting.

Ideally, the doorknocker should be a recipient who is both committed to and knowledgeable about welfare rights and whose face is familiar to the potential membership. Such a woman encounters only minimal suspicion and her word is accepted; she has lived through the same experiences as the potential members and she can speak the same language.

Unfortunately, none of the recipients in Pilgrim City had had any practical experience with welfare rights. Each one had to be taught; no one was ready to teach. (In those instances in which a larger group was subdividing, this difficulty never arose since members of the existing group both lived in the neighborhood and were knowledgeable about the organization and thus formed a natural pool of doorknockers.)

The Pilgrim City problem could have been dealt with by recruiting members of existing welfare rights affiliates to serve as doorknockers. But the drive organizer rejected this alternative because he valued the familiar face of a neighborhood recipient more than any details of what might be said. In addition, the organizer hoped that the future lay leadership of the group could be chosen from among the experienced doorknockers, which possibility would be eliminated if doorknockers from outside the area were used.

The MWRO organizers were well equipped to make a skillful presentation of the required material, but it was not always easy for a young, white, middle-class, college-aged staff member to win the confidence or communicate his message to the welfare recipient. In part, these difficulties were overcome through training. Organizers were taught to use simple language but to avoid condescending attempts to use lower-class vocabulary or grammar. Similarly, the organizers were urged to avoid both sloppy clothing and business suits. (The long-haired male organizer in bell bottom trousers or bluejeans was likely to be suspected of being a hippie or SDS member. An organizer would be rendered equally ineffective by dressing in tie and jacket, which would thus create suspicion that he was a Welfare Department investigator.)

The Boston model solved the dilemma of strengths and weaknesses of both organizers and recipients by stipulating that doorknocking teams consist of one recipient and one organizer. Ideally, the recipient member of the team would do all the talking. In the more usual case, both members of the team shared the responsibility. At first, the organizers said practically everything. But as recipients gained experience and confidence, the organizers confined themselves to adding those things that the recipient had forgotten or misstated.

The recipient members of the Pilgrim City doorknocking teams were recruited in a variety of ways. As indicated above, some were asked to help out after discussions at the recruiting table in the supermarket. The drive organizer sought recommendations from members of existing welfare rights affiliates who had friends or relatives on welfare in Pilgrim City. All women from Pilgrim City who had previously called the MWRO statewide headquarters with requests for information or assistance were asked to take part in the organizing drive. Finally, a few doorknockers were chosen from among the most enthusiastic recipients contacted by other doorknockers.

Although attempts were made to gain the assistance of clergymen and antipoverty workers, the prime source of non-recipient "organizer" members of the doorknocking teams was the MWRO staff. Participation in an organizing drive was an initiation rite for everyone joining the MWRO staff and demonstration of skill on these drives became the major basis for advancement within that staff. The neophyte staff member who worked well under two or three drive organizers could expect to become a drive organizer himself in the near future. Those who became central office administrators in the MWRO often welcomed the opportunity to escape temporarily from routine officework and spend some time "on the doors." Although welfare rights organizers elsewhere in the country sometimes made extensive use of housewives and part-time student volunteers to aid in recruiting, the MWRO avoided the use of such "amateurs" wherever possible.

"Doorknocking"—The First Contact with Potential Members

The Boston model prescribed each aspect of the initial contact with potential members down to the smallest detail; nothing was left to chance. The extremes to which this planning was refined can be illustrated by the detailed instructions as to the preferred procedure for (literally) knocking on doors. According to the model, the non-recipient should knock on the door and then quickly step aside. Experience had shown that if the recipients knocked, they often did so timidly or not loudly enough, and the potential member was unsure whether anyone were outside her door. The non-recipient was taught to move quickly aside in case the potential member looked out through her peephole.

If she saw a stranger, she might not open her door; if she saw a friend or at least a familiar face, the reception would be more likely to be a warm one.

The speech that MWRO doorknockers gave to potential members—irrevently called "the pitch" by the staff—was perhaps the most elaborately developed aspect of the Boston model. There were, of course, idiosyncratic differences in delivery and emphasis by different doorknockers. But a prime objective in training doorknockers was to reduce these idiosyncracies and to present the carefully honed performance as closely approximating the paradigm as possible

Most elements of the pitch had been developed to deal with one of three basic functions: creating an image of the local group as a sure-fire source of tangible benefits, minimizing feelings of fear, suspicion, and apathy among potential members, and giving enough information so that none of the events at either the first meeting or first confrontation would come as a surprise to those in attendance and hence create a disturbance. Although the pitch included a formal description of the welfare rights movement—its goals, its structure, and the like—the MWRO staff recognized that such abstractions were difficult to communicate in an initial interview. They therefore relied on repetition of the pitch at meetings and on the distribution of NWRO pamphlets to supplement the sketchy understanding of welfare rights that most women gained during their first contact with MWRO doorknockers.

The key to the success of the organizing drive was the ability of the doorknockers to convince people that they could get furniture if, and only if, they joined the Pilgrim City Welfare Rights Organization. This was accomplished by showing the potential member a mimeographed form containing the state-approved furniture guidelines. Invariably, the potential member lacked at least several items on this list, and the doorknockers stressed that she was entitled to these items and could get them—by coming to the first meeting of the PCWRO to get the request forms and then by going to the welfare office to hand them in. If she did this, the furniture would be hers within two weeks.

After showing the list to the potential member, the doorknocking team immediately took it back; if the form were to be left with the recipient, she might fill it out herself and thus have no further need for the welfare rights organization. "If you want the table and chairs," the woman was told, "come to the meeting and get the forms."

Leaving the lists with recipients would have been consistent with a general goal of improving the lot of the welfare mothers and with the strategy of creating a financial crisis through ever-increasing welfare appropriations as outlined by Cloward and Piven. Such a strategy was used to some degree in New York City. But the Boston model recognized neither providing individualized assistance to people with problems—"social work" as it is disdainfully called by the MWRO staff—nor creating a fiscal crisis as legitimate goals. Instead it sought to promote the mobilization of welfare mothers into powerful organizations.

Thus, once a woman was sold on the value of forms, they were quickly taken away from her.

In the Pilgrim City case, when potential members seemed doubtful as to whether the PCWRO could deliver on its promises, the doorknockers were ready to cite specific provisions of Welfare Department regulations and give examples of nearby welfare rights organizations whose members had recently won special needs grants for furniture.

In some instances, recipients, who were interested in the furniture after hearing about it, brought up individual problems they were having with the Welfare Department. Doorknockers were taught to reply to all but the most extreme individual emergencies with the following:

> *I can't help you with this problem right now, but when you have*
> *a strong local group, you will be able to deal with these situations. . . .*
> *As a matter of fact, once the Pilgrim City Welfare Rights Organization*
> *gets on its feet, problems like this won't even arise any more.*

Limitations of time and manpower made it impossible for members of the door-knocking teams to help recipients with their idiosyncratic problems and still meet a large number of recipients during the short, intense organizing drive. New MWRO organizers often found this a difficult lesson to learn: they were community organizers and not supplementary caseworkers.

Many of those contacted by Pilgrim City doorknockers were afraid of getting involved in the kind of militant activities they associated with previous MWRO activity. The doorknockers were taught to deal with these fears in several ways. In the first place, efforts were made during this initial contact—and during the first meeting as well—to avoid any inflammatory words. When the agenda for the first meeting and first confrontation was discussed, there was no mention of "demonstrations," "confrontations," or even "marches." Instead, more neutral words were employed:

> *At the first meeting, the group will "go down" to the welfare*
> *office, to "introduce" the newly elected officers of the Pilgrim City*
> *Welfare Rights Organization, and to "hand in" the furniture request*
> *forms.*

Recipients who were still hesitant to associate themselves with such militants as "those crazy ladies from Roxbury" were told that each MWRO affiliate would be autonomous:

> *The PCWRO will be your own group. It will do only what you*
> *and the members vote to do; no one else can impose their will upon*
> *you. No one is forced to take part in statewide actions if they don't*
> *want to. In addition, the PCWRO will be entitled to send its own*

*representatives to all MWRO meetings and thus have a major influence
on the future of welfare rights in Massachusetts.*

At times, doorknockers would also try to defend the "crazy ladies":

> *Those ladies are a lot like you. They didn't want to get involved
> but their children needed beds and clothing and they vowed not to
> leave the welfare office until they got it. It's only because of the
> actions of people like those ladies in Roxbury that furniture and
> clothing are available to you today.*

In the event that a woman raised the possibility of arrests following welfare
rights activity, the doorknockers would parry such thrusts as follows:

> *No one in the welfare rights movement is ever arrested without
> having decided in advance to do so. Whenever it looks like there is
> a real chance of arrests—and the police always give several warnings—
> the group takes a vote on what to do. If a majority votes to stay and
> risk arrest, only those who voted yes are expected to stay. If a major-
> ity votes no, then everyone leaves. And besides this, no one arrested
> has ever been in jail for more than an hour to two. We have excellent
> lawyers and you don't have to worry.*

Many of the women remained hesitant and expressed fears of alienating the
caseworkers whom they felt had been so good to them. The doorknockers had
an answer for this one, too. First they brought out the form with the furniture
guidelines a second time, and asked:

> *Did your caseworker ever show you a list like this? Why do you
> think he didn't? Welfare rights tells people everything they are
> entitled to. Social workers never do.*

If this was not sufficient, the doorknockers then attacked the imputation of
caseworker generosity by stressing the concept of welfare as a right:

> *OK, so Mr. Snow did get you a new chair for the living room. But
> he gave it to you because it was yours by right, because you were
> entitled to it, not because he was being nice to you or doing you a
> favor.*

Potential members' fears of reprisals were sometimes alleviated by showing
letters from Welfare Department officials telling of a recipient's right to belong
to any group she chooses without losing her welfare benefits. In Pilgrim City,
the welfare officials were accommodating and agreed to include such a statement
with all welfare checks sent out shortly before the campaign had begun.

If a recipient persisted in the belief that her social worker was the best any-one could hope for, the doorknockers countered with the observation that "good social workers don't last," and even if this one were good, there was no guarantee that the next one wouldn't be terrible. The recipient doorknocker buttressed this line of argument:

> As for me, I've had five different workers in the past two years. You just can't depend on getting a good one. What you really need is power.

Finally the wavering recipient was confronted with an idea she had never previously considered, did she really need a caseworker at all:

> What you really need is money, not social workers. Just because you are poor, you don't need a social worker to tell you how to live. Who knows more about living in a housing project, you or her? And who knows more about bringing up children, you or a twenty-year-old virgin college graduate? Welfare rights says you should have adequate income without having to submit to investigations each time you ask for something. If you want a social worker, you should be free to ask for one. But otherwise, they should stay out of your life. . . .

Negative attitudes of the prospective members were somewhat neutralized through non-verbal means as well as through the pitch. For example, the professional looking stationery of the initial mailing and the membership pins and organizational newspapers shown by the doorknockers helped to convey an image of the welfare rights movement as a large respectable and powerful force in American society, which thus helped to counteract feelings of apathy.

According to the Boston model, the best way to insure that everything at the first meeting would occur as planned was to prepare the membership in advance. For example, if women were not told about the necessity to pay dues, some of them might become irritable and question whether the door-knockers had been any more honest than their caseworkers; if warned in advance, virtually no one would complain about paying to join the local group. Doorknockers were thus instructed to say:

> The National Welfare Rights Organization is a nationwide group of people just like you. Welfare policy is made on all levels of govern-ment, and if we want to affect anything that happens in Washington, we need a nationwide organization. Membership in the NWRO is one dollar per year and dues will be collected at the first meeting of the PCWRO. In terms of building up an organization to represent you in Washington, you really get your dollar's worth. Besides, for just one dollar you get a membership button just like the one I'm wearing and copies of the NWRO newsletter just like this one here.

The MWRO staff attached a great deal of value to the welfare rights dues structure. By paying dues, a member could think of herself as having made some contribution towards the growth of her group.

The dues structure of the welfare rights movement has also been useful in lobbying activities. It has enabled welfare rights leaders to claim to be speaking for a number of dues-paying members rather than any supposed following. Furthermore, although the dues make up only a tiny fraction of the NWRO budget, the existence of membership dues provides an effective debating point whenever the leadership is challenged as to the source of its funds.

In addition to a discussion of dues, the PCWRO doorknockers also concentrated upon describing the other events of the first meeting:

> *Shortly after you get to the meeting, everyone will fill out the furniture request forms that we just showed you and some appeal forms—just in case. After that, there will be elections for "temporary" officers and people will be able to volunteer for the grievance committee. Members of the grievance committee will be trained to help the other members of the PCWRO whenever they run into difficulty with their caseworkers.*
>
> *After the forms are filled out, everyone will go down to the welfare office to introduce the newly elected officers to Mr. Evil, the office director, so that he knows he is now dealing with a group, and then we'll hand in the forms we just filled out.*

The use of the future tense in this part of the pitch shows how the Boston model attempted to give the MWRO staff control over the first meeting by presenting the agenda and the subsequent march to the welfare office as accomplished facts rather than decisions to be made by the membership. When these attempts were successful, the membership never realized that there were decisions that might have been made contrary to the advance plans.

Although most of the pitch consisted of efforts to personalize the campaign in terms of individual needs, to counteract negative attitudes, and to present the agenda for the first meeting, some of it represented straightforward attempts to communicate the ideology of the movement and the role of political power in bringing about social change:

> *The reason welfare is so bad is because welfare recipients are not organized. One by one they can't get what they need because they have no power—and that's what this country responds to, power.*
>
> *There are three kinds of power. The first is money power. We can't have that kind of power because we have no money—the Welfare Department doesn't give us enough to live on. If we had money power, we wouldn't need the group so badly.*
>
> *The second kind of power is the power of numbers. If we organize and get our people together, we can have that power to get what we need.*

> *We will have this power at our first meeting, and we have numbers to back us up in the Massachusetts Welfare Rights Organization and the National Welfare Rights Organization.*
>
> *The third kind of power is the power of the vote. We haven't used this power yet, but when we get organized, we can develop this power and also have a major statewide impact.*

The doorknockers were instructed to tell the potential members: "If we organize, we can have the power to get what we need—*and* to change the whole rotten welfare system." The pitch was ambiguous as to the relative priorities of "getting what we need" and "changing the system"; while the broader goal was mentioned, it seemed somewhat like an afterthought. Questions of political power to change the welfare system were uppermost in the minds of the MWRO staff, but they realized this could not be communicated in a short pitch.

Many of the elements of the pitch served more than one function. The seemingly straightforward description of the structure and functioning of the welfare rights movement was designed to emphasize its power and further combat apathy. If a recipient could be convinced that thousands of others had already joined, she might feel less ashamed to admit publicly that she was on welfare and therefore be more willing to make a commitment to the PCWRO:

> *The NWRO has local affiliates across the country all working to change the welfare system. There are over 30,000 members organized in local neighborhoods, in big cities and even on a statewide basis. We might be able to get a little more money by forming our own local group, but no one can hope to change anything important unless she is linked together with the other groups from across the country.*
>
> *The NWRO is fighting for an adequate income, enough money to live on, for welfare recipients all over the U.S.A. This means black and white, old and young, urban and rural—people in Alabama and Mississippi, in the slums, ghettos and barrios everywhere. People in Worcester have already gotten school clothing for their children, and on the Cape many people are getting supplementary rent payments. If they can do it in Worcester and on the Cape, in Chicago and New York, Alabama and Alaska—then we can surely do it in Pilgrim City!*

After completing this pitch, the members of the doorknocking team spent a minute or two in informal discussion with the potential member. Before going, the doorknockers left a pamphlet describing the NWRO and a leaflet giving the time and place for the first meeting. If the contact had taken place in an apartment building, the team left additional leaflets on the walls and entry tables. Before going on to the next address on their list, the doorknockers recorded their impressions of the visit on a three-by-five card that would eventually go into the permanent files of the MWRO.

The initial contact was followed up by either another leaflet or a postcard timed to arrive a day or two before the first meeting. On the day of the meeting and on the night before, the Pilgrim City drive organizer and a few other MWRO staff members tried to call those recipients on their lists who had telephones to make one final effort to coax people to attend. Once that was completed, they could only await the meeting itself.

The First Meeting

Although every element of the organizing drive until this point was directed towards maximizing the turnout at the first meeting of the Pilgrim City Welfare Rights Organization, the success of the meeting was not measured solely in terms of total attendance. The first meeting could be considered successful only if it were followed by a successful demonstration at the welfare office. The meeting itself was only an intermediate—albeit crucial—step along the way.

For this reason, the Boston model called for strict control of the first meeting by the drive organizer and his staff. Regardless of how the drive organizer personally felt about the virtues of participatory democracy, the MWRO staff director had taught him that there would never be an organization to be run democratically unless the first confrontation ended successfully, and in order to ensure that end result, nothing could be left to chance. Thus while the appearance of democratic decision-making was desirable, the full reality had to be postponed until the new group was on its feet. Wherever possible those attending the first meeting would be presented with accomplished facts and not asked to make decisions. If members sought a larger role, the drive organizer would agree only if he felt it would not jeopardize the success of the meeting and confrontation.

Although the new members were not given a direct role to play, this does not mean that the drive organizer was free to do whatever he pleased at the first meeting. Control by organizers required acquiescence by members, and thus the MWRO staff was constrained to choose courses of action that made demands the members considered acceptable.

In order to delineate this zone of indifference and determine just how far the members could be pushed, MWRO staff spent every free minute at the first meetings conversing informally with the members. In each conversation, the organizers tried to make a personal assessment of what could be expected of the member: how much of the theory of welfare rights did she understand, would she be willing to remain in a sit-in situation if arrests were threatened, and so forth.

Virtually every detail of the first meeting was planned to minimize independent decision-making by the membership. Even such items as the time for which the meeting was called had a complicated rationale: The first meeting of the Pilgrim City Welfare Rights Organization was called for 10:30 in the morning because there were problems with almost every other possibility. Had the meeting been scheduled for the evening (as were the early MWRO meetings) the first confrontation could not take place until the next morning thereby giving each member eight or ten hours for second thoughts. Had the meeting been scheduled for early or mid-afternoon, the confrontation might not have been successfully completed by the five o'clock closing time for welfare offices which would thus force the issue of abandoning the effort or risking arrest for trespassing. Had the meeting gotten underway too late in the morning, the members arriving at the welfare office would discover their caseworkers out to lunch and thus be faced with the decision whether they should wait an hour or two to see them. An early morning meeting would have eliminated these problems, but if the meeting began too early, many women would arrive late and miss the beginning of the carefully orchestrated presentation. Mid-morning was the only time left.

Although the meeting was not scheduled to begin for nearly an hour, several of those contacted by the doorknockers were already in the chuch meeting hall when the Pilgrim City drive organizer arrived to begin decorating the stage with MWRO posters proclaiming the goal of *"More Money Now."* Soon after this, the recipient members of the doorknocking team began to arrive. In order to further the impression that recipients were running the meeting, these door-knockers were quickly pressed into service greeting other recipients as they arrived. One was chosen to take the name and address of everyone coming through the door in order to form a group mailing list. Another stood nearby to collect the one dollar dues and help fill out membership cards. A third woman was asked to give out membership pins as soon as the dues had been paid, while a fourth was recruited to distribute furniture request forms and an agenda for the meeting. (The decision to assign these tasks to the recipient door-knockers is thus evidence of the MWRO staff priority for reassuring the new-comers and avoiding the image of outside recruiters even if this meant a sacrifice in speed or accuracy.)

This procedure of stationing the recipient doorknockers at the entrance to the meeting room avoided giving potential members a chance to make any decisions on their own. Rather than listen to speeches and then decide whether to join, the prospective member was confronted by a dues-collector before she could pass through the doorway. Seeing that everyone inside had already paid, the newest arrival also paid her dues and became the newest member of the PCWRO.

By having the dues collected and a list of members drawn up before the meeting started, the drive organizer laid the foundation for rebuilding the PCWRO should anything unforeseen happen later. Even those who declined to accompany the group to the first confrontation were enrolled as members and could be easily reached to tell what transpired at the welfare office. Even reluctant members had acquired membership pins and some identification with the group, and the drive organizer got credit for recruiting them.

By distributing the furniture request forms immediately after the member had joined the organization, the Boston model provided for immediate gratification and a clearcut demonstration that the group was the source of the benefits. The drive organizer and other MWRO staff members circulated among the new members asking whether they needed any assistance in filling out the request forms. Often, the organizers ended up filling out the forms themselves. Members were asked to keep their completed request forms so that they could personally hand them to their own caseworkers which thus insured that they would go to the welfare office. At the same time, members were also given appeal forms—"just in case." These forms were not retained by the members but returned to the drive organizer; thus, should the furniture requests be denied, the PCWRO members would presumably have to come back to their group for further redress.

The mimeographed agenda was an effective device for foreclosing decisions. There was no question when the meeting would begin, who would run the meeting, or who would speak when. The agenda specified that officers would be elected only after introductory speeches had been completed. There would be no discussion about the name of the new group or whether it would decide to affiliate itself with any statewide or national organizations. The agenda stated it all quite clearly: this was the first meeting of the Pilgrim City Welfare Rights Organization, a local group of the MWRO and an affiliate of the NWRO. Several of the speakers would begin by welcoming the PCWRO "to the movement."

By 10:30, more than 50 women were seated in the meeting hall while others continued to stream in. (First meetings of MWRO local affiliates have been attended by as few as 8 members and as many as 500.) The process of signing up members and paying dues continued throughout the meeting and ended only when the group had left for the welfare office. Most of the women did not seem to know each other; they tended either to sit alone or perhaps in groups of two or three. About half of the women brought children along and the noise level in the hall rose sharply.

As soon as the drive organizer called the meeting to order, he introduced a priest to deliver an invocation. The group rose and bowed their heads as the priest began with the standard remarks about the "Father, Son, and Holy Ghost"; few seemed to notice as he shifted gears and began asking God's blessings for "those who came together to learn their rights and to fight for them." The combination of the priest's letter of endorsement of the drive, first meeting being held in the church, and the opening prayer proved to be a potent influence even upon non-Catholics in the new group.

Next on the agenda was a speech by a member of the MWRO Executive Board of lay leaders who expressed pleasure that the PCWRO had joined the movement and then briefly described the history of welfare rights activities in Massachusetts. The drive organizer then took the floor to repeat the highpoints of the pitch that all of those present had already heard in their own living rooms.

As was done during the doorknocking, subdued rhetoric was used throughout; the words "demonstration" and "march" were avoided. Those who later read about their involvement in a march or demonstration in a newspaper generally had one of two reactions. Some thought that the press as usual was exaggerating and began to wonder whether the stories about the "crazy ladies from Roxbury" were also exaggerations. Others began to realize that "if that was a demonstration, it wasn't so terrible after all." Either way, the PCWRO had won a member by reducing his apprehensions. (Those Pilgrim City recipients who had not been present had their fears increased by reports of demonstrations, which was another reason for maximizing the turnout at the first confrontation.) The trip to the welfare office just after the meeting was treated as an accomplished fact. It was simply the last item on the agenda:

> Go to the welfare office to introduce our new officers and our group to Mr. Evil, the office director, and to turn in the request forms to our caseworkers.

There was no vote on this tactic or even any discussion; all speakers simply assumed that it would happen that way. The only votes at the meeting were for the election of officers—and many of these were by acclamation.

Election of lay leaders was a critical step in increasing the group's legitimacy in future confrontations. The casual observer might have thought that this election was a relaxation of the tight control exercised by the drive organizer over the development of the PCWRO. In fact, the elections were influenced by the drive organizer and, at least in the short run, they produced merely the appearance of shared authority. The newly elected chairman of the PCWRO would repeat the plans for the first confrontation and stand in the forefront, but she had played little or no role in formulating the plans and was merely leading in their execution. Her lack of experience made her almost completely dependent upon the drive organizer for advice about how to proceed. She did not receive any encouragement from the organizer to use her own judgment in critical situations during the first meeting or ensuing confrontation.

The basic device used by the Boston model organizer to influence the elections at the first meeting, was the position of this item on the agenda. In MWRO first meetings, elections took place directly after the drive organizer introduced the recipient doorknockers who "had worked so hard to make this meeting possible and deserve lots of credit for it." Many of these same women had been greeting newcomers as they entered the hall and passing out membership pins and furniture request forms. These were women whom the drive organizer knew and with whom he knew could work. In a situation in which few of the new members knew each other in advance of the meeting and few had much experience in running for office since class elections in grade school, it was usually the case that those doorknockers praised by the drive organizer—and whose names were printed on the meeting agendas—would be elected to office. In Pilgrim City, the newly elected chairman was the first name on the list printed in the agenda and had been the first introduced by the drive organizer.

Some of those attending the first meeting might have been interested in being a leader or have had leadership potential, but they either had not been doorknockers or did not get elected for other reasons. In order to enable these people to play leadership roles in the future, the drive organizer announced and the agenda confirmed that those who had just been elected would serve only as "temporary" officers—although the term temporary was never defined. If those elected at the first meeting developed a sound relationship with both the members and organizers there might never be another election; if they did not develop such a relationship, "temporary" might turn out to mean a week or two. In addition to this, it was also announced (but never voted upon) that anyone volunteering for the "grievance committee" could be a member of the PCWRO Executive Committee with the same voting power as the elected officers. Non-electable mothers could thus still play an active role in governing the group while they built support for future elections.

With the elections completed, the drive organizer and newly elected chairman announced that it was time for the next part of the meeting— going to the welfare office to turn in the furniture forms. In order to minimize the chance for second thoughts on the part of the members, everyone was quickly directed from the hall (through the only unlocked door) to buses waiting outside that would carry the group to the Pilgrim City welfare office. Had transportation not been available, the drive organizer might have sacrificed the benefits of a church meeting hall in favor of one much closer to the welfare office in order to minimize the possibility of "dropping out" by making the march as short as possible.

Before they fully realized what was happening, the new members were swept up by the emotion of the moment and on their way to the first confrontation. The first meeting had been a success.

The relationship of a group and its organizer is one of the critical issues in the field of community organization. Some community organizers would object to some aspects of the Boston model first meeting as described above. Even within the welfare rights movement, some organizers placed a considerably higher priority on the nurturing of indigenous leadership than did the MWRO. Holders of this viewpoint sought to reduce or eliminate the need for non-recipient organizers as soon as was possible and thus favored maximizing the decision-making role of the lay leadership. Many of them set up "organizing committees" of welfare recipients early in their recruitment drives and immediately began sharing decision-making power with this group. Their first meetings were chaired by such organizing committees.

As already indicated, the Boston model rejected such delegation of power to members of the organization because of its belief in the paramount value of completing the first confrontation successfully. Any one of a hundred bad judgments by newly elected, inexperienced, and untrained lay leaders could jeopardize that success and thus decision-making power had to remain largely in the hands of the drive organizer. Until the first meeting of the Pilgrim City Welfare Rights Organization, no welfare recipient had the right to speak for the membership; the recipient doorknockers were never consulted in planning the drive. Although the meetings of the PCWRO were chaired by a member of the MWRO Executive Board, effective control of the meeting remained in the hands of the drive organizer. The unspoken syllogism for MWRO organizing drives was a cold-blooded one: If there is no successful first confrontation, there will be no group. Before you have a democratically run group, you need a group. Therefore democracy must be (temporarily) postponed.

Organizer dominance was thus a crucial principle in a Boston model first meeting. Whenever anything appeared to be going badly, the drive organizer would reject the standardized meeting agenda and improvise to deal with the difficulty in the manner most likely to ensure the success of the first confrontation. Thus, for example, when meetings run late and the election of officers began to get bogged down, the drive organizer was expected to try to abort the election process after only two or three officers were chosen. This would maintain the momentum of the meeting, and to avoid the situation in which caseworkers would be out to lunch when the first confrontation began. In one case, the first meeting appeared to be disintegrating because of a disturbance caused by a rival organization, and the drive organizer postponed the entire election until the group had left the disrupters behind and arrived at the welfare office.

Although the agenda for the first meetings of the early affiliates of the MWRO had contained an item "Questions and tell it like it is," the questions were sometimes embarassing and were later discouraged by eliminating this item from the agenda. Whenever difficult questions were raised, an experienced MWRO organizer would not hesitate to interrupt whoever was speaking in order to handle the question in the best way possible. If the question "wasn't the welfare rights movement really encouraging people to ask for more than they really needed" appeared to be giving the drive organizer some trouble, a more experienced colleague who had been quietly seated in the rear observing the proceedings would come forward and begin cautiously but firmly, "May I say something on that point?" He would not wait for an answer but immediately began giving a pep talk to counteract any doubts being raised by the questionners.

The First Confrontation

With the first meeting successfully completed, the climax of the organizing drive began. A victory at the welfare office that entailed the distribution of material benefits would prove the credibility of the drive organizer's promises, cement the loyalty of those present at the confrontation, and serve as a major selling point in future drives for new members. Violence or arrests at the first confrontation—and no benefits—would confirm the worst fears of the new members and those who had been holding back. It could easily mean the destruction of the new group before it had ever gotten off the ground. The crucial decision in a first confrontation, then, was how far should the welfare office personnel be pushed? Some militancy would be needed, but while the group needed a victory—or at least an event which could be defined to the members as a victory—it was vital that welfare office personnel not be pushed to the point of exasperation at which they would order the arrest of the demonstrators.

According to the Boston model, it was the job of the drive organizer to strike the delicate balance necessary to assure a victory without seriously risking total disaster. The skill (or perhaps the artistry) of the organizer was thus put to perhaps its most severe test in determining when the group should withdraw from the field of battle to count its booty. This task was complicated by the organizer's desire to remain dominant despite his wish to give the impression that the newly elected lay leaders were running the demonstration.

While the members of the Pilgrim City Welfare Rights Organization were travelling from the church meeting hall to the welfare office, the drive organizer sought out the newly elected chairman of the group and described in detail what was likely to occur and how she should react to the various responses that the welfare office director might make. The organizer conveyed an accurate picture of how events would develop and the new chairman proved able to rise to the occasion, which enabled the organizer to remain in the background throughout the demonstration. But he would have seriously considered stepping forward at any point if things had appeared to be going badly. Here as elsewhere, the Boston model stressed insuring successful execution over lay leadership development through trial and error.

The PCWRO began winning victories from the moment the members first entered the welfare office. Many recipients felt that they were indeed noticed as they entered and that they were getting some form of immediate response. Some members thought they saw discomfort or even fear on the part of their caseworkers. Thus, even before the first demands were made, many saw (what was interpreted to them as) evidence of the power that comes from being a member of a welfare rights organization.

The first PCWRO demand was to see the office director, ostensibly to introduce the group and its newly elected lay leaders. The quick appearance of the director was seen by the PCWRO members as another demonstration of the power of their group. Few were accustomed to seeing their own caseworker within what they had considered a reasonable amount of time; they

had never dreamt of trying to see the director. Now within a few minutes of
their arrival he came forward to negotiate with them.

The director's first reaction to the group was excessive politeness:

> Oh Mrs. Jones, I'm so glad to hear about the formation of your
> new group and that you were elected chairman. But you know of
> course that you don't need to form organizations to get what you are
> entitled to in this office. You and everyone in your group should
> know that you should feel free to come to me personally if any of
> you ever run into any difficulties.

In the course of the welcoming speech, the director ran through the clinches
of his profession and concluded with the idea that "the entire staff of this office
has no other job than to serve the recipients and meet their needs."

The impromptu welcoming speech represented yet another victory by adding
to the legitimacy of the organization in the minds of its members. First of all,
it indicated formal recognition of the group as representing Pilgrim City recipients by the Welfare Department hierarchy. The displays of respect and deference given by the PCWRO chairman—even if they sometimes verged on sarcasm
and mock deference—presented a welcome change to the members, a change
for which the new group received credit.

But despite the importance of these symbolic victories, the Boston model
required distribution of tangible benefits. Thus although the welfare office
director attempted to continue with the pleasantries, the PCWRO chairman, with
some coaching from the drive organizer, pressed to enter into direct negotiations
on the requests for special needs grants for furniture for the group. At first, the
director pointed out the impossibility of carrying out meaningful discussions
with such a large body of people crowded into a narrow reception area. "Wouldn't
you prefer to appoint a delegation to meet with me in my office?" the director
asked. "Then we can report our decisions to your members." The chairman,
who had been forewarned of this ploy, refused to accept it on the grounds that
she wanted all of her members to see what was going on.

The Boston model called for rejecting the appointment of a delegation for
a number of reasons. The local group's chief bargaining chip was intimidation;
this advantage would have been dissipated had the director been able to escape
facing the threatening mob. Secondly, there was the danger of a sell-out by
leaders if they met privately with the director. Finally, if a delegation were
appointed, it would have been improper for the drive organizer to have been
chosen and thus he would no longer be able to keep abreast of developments
and advise the lay leaders. The problem of keeping up the interest of those
not on the negotiating team and the perceived need for each member to witness
the power of the group with her own eyes were further reasons behind the
demand that all negotiations be carried out in the open.

Although the Pilgrim City welfare office director gave in on this demand after a short but heated discussion, had the drive organizer felt that the director would not do so, he would have disregarded all of the above arguments and encouraged the chairman to agree to the appointment of such a delegation. Any victory was more important than risking arrest before the negotiations even got under way.

The physical setting for the negotiations in the Pilgrim City welfare office was ideal from the point of view of the drive organizer: an increasingly distaught director standing in the midst of an increasingly tense group of welfare recipients was subjected to an escalating stream of invective and harassment from the general membership as he attempted to negotiate on the demands for furniture. According to the Boston model, victory would be assured if the director could be brought to the point of giving concessions just to get the noisy unruly group out of his office.

As soon as one member interrupted the general negotiations to tell the director of some personal problem with her caseworker, there was no need for further instigation on the part of welfare rights organizers. Virtually every member of the PCWRO had some complaint of her own, and nearly everyone in the group found some point at which to make complaints during this first opportunity to talk with the welfare office director. Although the director attempted to restrict his conversation to negotiations with the chairman, this proved impossible. Whenever he sought to limit the distractions by agreeing with a complaining member and suggesting that they talk the matter over in private at some later time. Others were encouraged to come forward and seek the same treatment.

Saul Alinsky has suggested that the function of the community organizer should be to rub raw the sores of discontent and to "agitate to the point of conflict."[2] The Boston model first confrontation was designed so that welfare recipients stimulated each other to enter into shouting matches with caseworkers and directors without any input from organizers. But the drive organizer, other MWRO staff members, and lay leaders from other groups circulated among the PCWRO members throughout the confrontation interpreting what was happening, prompting statements of indignation from the members and occasionally delivering a powerful stream of invective themselves. A dramatic highlight of the confrontation came when the welfare office director attempted to isolate the members from what he suspected was a group of outside agitators. Unfortunately for him, he happened to single out a lay leader of another MWRO affiliate rather than an organizer and so when he asked the heckler "Are you on welfare?" he was answered with a resounding "Yes!"

The confusion escalated as the children accompanying some members became restless. A few began milling around, yelling and screaming. Others attempted to play with the telephones and typewriters. One or two caseworkers tried to amuse the children and play with them; a number of their colleagues gathered around to watch. Before long, all work in the Pilgrim City welfare office came to a halt.

Since he needed a quick victory, the drive organizer had chosen a demand that was widely recognized as legitimate by Welfare Department officials—special needs grants for furniture. There was no doubt that recipients who needed furniture were entitled to supplementary welfare checks to buy them. The critical issue, then, and thus the major item of contention in the negotiations between the PCWRO chairman and the director, was whether everyone in the group could prove the need for those things being demanding.

On some occasions, welfare office directors agreed to accept the word of welfare rights demonstrators that they truly needed everything for which they were asking. But in this case, the welfare office director refused to compromise on the principle that individual need would have to be verified through personal interviews between each recipient and her caseworker. When the director said that no benefits could be distributed until after caseworkers had visited the homes of each member to verify their needs, the PCWRO chairman, who was ready for this, responded:

> *We claim we need the goods. Isn't that enough for you or don't you trust us? Don't you believe me when I say we don't have enough beds? Didn't your caseworker notice that we have two beds for four children the last time he was in my home?*

Once the issue had been put in these terms, the director could only lose. If he agreed to accept the word of the recipients--something that his caseworkers had never done before—he was clearly demonstrating the power of the group and his own susceptibility to pressure tactics. If he did not agree—which was the more common response—his refusal served to build greater hostility between recipient and caseworker. As hotility grew, so did the readiness of the membership to participate in militant actions.

After another heated discussion, the chairman of the PCWRO acquiesced to a demand for home visits to verify needs. But even this was turned into a minor victory by demanding that caseworkers make appointments in advance of home visits. Most members had never thought of asking for appointments in the past; it brought them satisfaction as the welfare director accepted the demand.

The chairman pressed for a deadline by which all the home visits would be completed so that the group could return to the office and pick up their checks together. According to this "pick-up date" strategy, the chairman told the director that the entire group would return in two weeks to collect their checks. The beauty of this strategy was that even if the group had to withdraw from the confrontation empty-handed, they could claim victory in the imminent receipt of tangible benefits. Nearly everyone who attended the first PCWRO meeting and confrontation would come back to the second in order to pick up her check, and many others after hearing about this victory would join the group, which would ensure an even larger turnout at the second confrontation.

With the demand for furniture resolved, attention shifted to the specific circumstances of each member's request, and the welfare office director stated that each of those who brought a request form would have to see her caseworker to discuss the requests and perhaps make an appointment for a home visit. The interviews with individual caseworkers also gave an opportunity for the members to seek resolution of other demands and idiosyncratic grievances. The director was permitted to escape at this point, and the single confrontation broke down into a number of smaller ones. While the bulk of the group waited less than patiently in the reception area, a handful of PCWRO members began their individual confrontations with caseworkers.

Normally, recipients of public welfare make requests of their caseworkers without any assistance. At the first confrontation—and at all future ones—the drive organizers offered to have either a MWRO staff member or another recipient attend the interview as an advocate. Whenever a caseworker refused to admit such a third person to the interview, a quick visit to the welfare office director or a telephone call to the Welfare Department regional office soon affirmed the right of advocacy and provided the PCWRO with another victory.

The role of the MWRO organizer in these individual confrontations was much broader than that which might normally have been played by a lawyer or a more traditional advocate; he spent as much time trying to win the loyalty of the member and to demonstrate that the group was a crucial link between members' needs and their fulfillment as he did in seeking to convince the caseworker. While a tangible victory remained the ultimate aim, the organizer-as-advocate never missed an opportunity to demonstrate that caseworkers could be influenced by a combination of knowledge of one's rights and a willingness to fight for them or to continue the attack on recipient apathy by demonstrating that caseworkers were neither all-knowing nor all-powerful—and clearly not all-giving.

The MWRO organizer was also unlike a traditional advocate by his constant jumping from one interview to another, putting in a word or two, and then moving on to the next case. From time to time, he returned to the reception area to tell those who were waiting what was happening in an effort to maintain their interest and prevent the dwindling away of the group (and hence its coercive potential). Sometimes, he invited a few of those waiting to witness one or two interviews for themselves. At all times, the organizer was willing to alienate caseworkers in order to prove to the members that he was not afraid of anyone who worked for the Welfare Department. If a member could not be interviewed because her caseworker was not in the office, the organizer would take several members with him to the welfare director's office and demand:

Where is Mrs. Smith's caseworker? Why is she never around when people need her? Are you sure she isn't out shopping? Ok, if she isn't around why don't you approve the check yourself?

Although he never showed any sympathy for the plight of Welfare Department personnel himself, the organizer was always seeking to find caseworkers and supervisors who appeared sympathetic to the group. Hopefully, these sympathizers would be useful to the group in future demonstrations.

The tenor of the first confrontation changed when a member suddenly became hysterical and began screaming louder and louder that she would attack her caseworker if he didn't give in to her. The drive organizer quickly sought to draw as many members as possible into the hallway directly outside this caseworker's office to witness what was transpiring and to add to the intimidation. As both the organizer and other members began crowding into the tiny interview room in support of the hysterical woman, the caseworker decided to concede and grant her demands to avoid provoking anyone to commit violence.

Soon after this dramatic victory, other caseworkers began making concessions. As each member won redress of a grievance or a tangible benefit, the organizer invited her to report back to the group and to "testify" to this effect in interviews with other caseworkers and members: "If I got it, why can't everyone?" The drive organizer pressed for some victory for each of the members: if not a check, then a commitment to produce one by a certain deadline; if not a tangible benefit, then the settlement of some troublesome grievance. Whenever any member won anything, her report to the others whetted their appetites for more.

After a while, those women whose demands had already been met began to straggle out of the welfare office, but the drive organizer tried to persuade them to stay until everyone had been satisfied so that the pressure would be kept at a high pitch until the end of the confrontation. In addition to this, the Boston model organizer preferred a more formal closing of the first confrontation, so that he would have an opportunity to define what had just happened in a manner that would build gratitude and loyalty to the newly formed welfare rights organization.

The decision about whether and when to make the final speech, like all other important ones that preceded, it was made primarily by the drive organizer although it was now made in consultation with the newly elected local group chairman. The chairman and the drive organizer both made the same points in addressing the members: the group had won a number of impressive victories that day and those victories could be attributed primarily to the strength of numbers that the group provided. The final announcement was that the second meeting of the Pilgrim City Welfare Rights Organization would take place in two weeks at the church and that right after that meeting, everyone would return to the welfare office to pick up their furniture checks.

With the completion of the final speech, the charter members of the PCWRO left the welfare office and drifted off in various directions to return to their homes. The caseworkers started to restore the office to its previous state of repair and to process the forms required to meet the demands made

by the group. The drive organizer and other members of the MWRO staff
returned to the statewide storefront headquarters to begin their analyses of the
Pilgrim City organizing drive and how it might have been improved.

Several months had passed since the decision to build an MWRO affiliate
in Pilgrim City. It had been several weeks since the first teams began knocking
on doors. Only several hours had elapsed since the first recipient entered the
church meeting hall. But as the last recipient left the welfare office, the job
of building that group was completed. The Boston model had once again been
validated in the eyes of the MWRO staff, and a new welfare rights group had
been born.

4 Difficulties in Local Group Maintenance

The Boston model organizing drives almost invariably produced successful first meetings and first confrontations. But few of the local groups created in those drives were able to maintain their momentum—or their membership—for very long. Despite a spectacular birth and a vigorous youth consisting of well-attended meetings and militant demonstrations, the typical MWRO affiliate soon moved into a period of doldrums, marked by a loss of interest by the general membership, and then moved towards a lingering death. The life cycle was a relatively short one; within a year of its founding, the Pilgrim City Welfare Rights Organization comprised little more than a dozen or two activists and a mailing list. By July 1970, only a handful of the MWRO local affiliates were still meeting somewhat regularly and participating in coordinated activities with other groups in the state.

For most of its history, the MWRO was able to disguise its inability to maintain local group strength by concentrating its efforts upon repeated Boston model organizing drives and thus constantly created new local groups to replace those that were falling by the wayside. These new groups helped to maintain the MWRO membership rolls, to provide the bulk of the participants in state-wide demonstrations, and to keep the welfare rights movement in the headlines.

The membership of MWRO affiliates nearly doubled between August 1969 and June 1970, and increased from 1623 to 3232 members. However, this increase was accomplished through an influx of over 2000 members from local groups that had been formed after August 1969, which made up for a net loss of nearly 400 members from the 28 groups that were already in existence at that time. Of these 28 older groups, all but 10 had fewer members in 1970 than in the year before.

This pattern of rapid decline in membership interest appears even more sharply with respect to active participation in welfare rights activities. The dues-paying membership always exceeded the number of individuals who could be counted upon to participate in any given welfare rights activity. The proportion of members who came only to one or two meetings and confrontations and then had no further contact with the movement is undoubtedly a substantial one. Although there was usually token representation from most local affiliates at MWRO statewide demonstrations, the vast majority of the participants were normally drawn from those groups organized in the preceding six months or from older groups revitalized through new membership drives. Of the 45 MWRO affiliates in existence in the spring of 1970 and for which accurate data is available, roughly one-third had no representatives at the 8 major statewide activities while another third participated in only one or two activities.

The MWRO dependence upon new members and new groups can also be illustrated by the changing composition of the MWRO statewide executive board. Of 5 temporary statewide officers elected at the October 1968 meeting at which the organization was founded, only 1 was re-elected at the first MWRO convention four months later, and she got married and left the state within a few months. Of 11 statewide officers elected in February 1969 or appointed to office shortly thereafter, only 7 were active one year later and only 3 were re-elected at the second statewide convention. (Two more of the 11 returned to active leadership after those who had defeated them resigned their posts.)

These considerations thus force a reassessment of the Boston model, which focused on the causes of the disintegration of the local groups that appeared to have begun so well. It is important, however, to remember that all voluntary associations have trouble attracting members to meetings and that the MWRO did better in terms of maintaining group strength than did welfare rights affiliates in many other major states. The magnitude of the MWRO decline was exaggerated by the extremely high initial turnouts.

Preliminary Explanations

The simplest explanation for the failure of the MWRO local groups to thrive is that the attention of the MWRO organizers was always directed towards new organizing drives where they could be guaranteed a tangible pay-off for their efforts in the form of a sizeable turnout. Once a local group had won a few quick victories, there was little that its organizer could do except try to repeat his successes and ward off decline. Leading a new organizing drive was a considerably more attractive possibility both from the local organizer's point of view and from that of Bill Pastreich—and his successors—as a chief organizer who placed a premium on maximizing the MWRO's membership rolls.

The withdrawal of the original local group organizer from a MWRO affiliate often meant the end of its existence as an active organization. In large part, this was due to the group's dependence upon the organizer, which was an integral part of the Boston model. For example, the Boston model principle of minimum demand meant that the lay leaders of MWRO affiliates quickly learned that their organizers could be depended upon to handle most of the tedious work required to insure turnout at meetings and demonstrations. Few lay leaders ever had to bother with preparing notices of meetings, mimeographing such notices, or even stamping or mailing them. Once the organizer left, there was no one with the necessary experience. The importance of input from an MWRO organizer for local group maintenance is illustrated by the 8 welfare rights activities undertaken by statewide organization in the spring of 1970. Of the 10 groups that participated in 5 or more of the 8, all but 1 had the attention of a full- or part-time organizer.

The contention that this weakness was related to the Boston model is supported by observing those few local groups that continued to function once the MWRO organizers had been withdrawn. At least 3 of these groups had lay leaders who had previously been leaders of the Mothers for Adequate Welfare (MAW) and thus had been exposed to an organizing model which gave them a broader conception of the leadership functions.

It was often impossible to find any staff member adequately able to replace the original organizer of a local group. This was a result of the general preference among the MWRO staff to build one's own group as well as the assertiveness of lay leaders who refused to give anyone but the organizer who had built their groups the degree of deference that most MWRO organizers felt necessary.

The failure to maintain local groups was therefore a direct result of the brilliant success of the Boston model organizing drives. In a statewide organization with limited funds to support staff, the staff director tended to place organizers where they were most likely to show dramatic results—and where they were most happy for precisely the same reason.

Despite the attractiveness of this explanation, it does not go far enough. Even those groups that retained the services of a MWRO organizer were unable to maintain the strength demonstrated at the first meetings and confrontations. The removal of an organizer generally spelled the end of a local group, but the presence of an organizer was not enough to prevent the decline. For a fuller explanation, we must return to the basic principles of the Boston model and a review of the incentives to which the general membership was responding.

The Limitations of Benefit-Related Strategies

Although the MWRO membership responded to a wide variety of inducements to participate in organizational activities, each of them had built-in limitations that eventually destroyed its effectiveness in promoting the long-range growth of local groups.

Beginning with the initial contact with MWRO doorknockers, the typical member looked towards the welfare rights movement as a vehicle for the acquisition of material benefits. In recognition of this fact, the primary strategy for local group maintenance was a direct extension of the organizing drives described in the previous chapter. The Boston model organizers' creativity was limited largely to conceiving new, special needs benefits and devising strategies to win Welfare Department acceptance of these benefits. Because of the discretion left to individual caseworkers and supervisors in defining when special needs grants could be given out, the MWRO staff was constantly trying to interpret these circumstances as broadly as possible and then gain the precedent of their acceptance by a wide number of caseworkers.

Massachusetts Welfare Department regulations once provided that supplementary benefits for recipients' telephone bills could be paid if anyone's "health or safety" was involved. For this purpose, MWRO organizers used the following argument:

> The housing projects and virtually all places where welfare recipients live are both unhealthy and unsafe. A telephone call to the police or a doctor could easily save a life under these circumstances. Therefore all welfare recipients should have supplementary grants to pay for telephone bills.

Had they succeeded in convincing more than one or two caseworkers of the validity of this argument, another organizing tool would have been born:

> *The Welfare Department is giving telephones to everyone living in the Pilgrim City housing project. Come and get your applications at the next meeting of the PCWRO, next Tuesday at 10:30 in the St. James Church.*

Similarly, when MWRO organizers discovered that Welfare Department regulations permitted special needs grants for winter clothing for those who had moved to the state from "warm climates," some used Xerox copies of a voucher for such clothing for a recent immigrant from Puerto Rico to convince members of local groups to demand winter clothing for themselves.

When all else failed, MWRO organizers sometimes opted to misinterpret regulations. For example, the public welfare manual contained provisions for special needs grants for "religious events" that occurred once in a person's lifetime, such as first communion or bar mitzvah. In the spring of 1969, the MWRO staff sought to apply this clause as a justification for a series of coordinated demonstrations demanding special needs grants for Easter clothing. The demands seemed reasonable enough to attract a sizeable turnout of members of existing welfare rights organizations as well as to motivate hundreds of new members to join.

The demands for telephones, winter coats for adults, and Easter clothing went largely unanswered. However, such demands elicited the participation of hundreds of members, and their rejection helped increase the hostility between the recipients and their caseworkers, which laid the groundwork for future militant actions.

Since the maintenance of credibility was vital to group maintenance, the MWRO organizers had to make sure that campaigns that were guaranteed of success were intermingled with those others. Isolated defeats could be explained by organizers as resulting from an inadequate turnout—"if only more mothers had showed up, then we could have won"—but if the members were to come back, material benefits would have to be provided fairly regularly.

According to this point of view, the ideal strategy for a local welfare rights affiliate was to adopt a "benefit-of-the-month club" strategy: an organizing drive built around the issue of furniture grants followed by a cycle of other special needs grant demands throughout the year. Such a cycle would include demands for supplementary welfare checks for back-to-school clothing in August and September, winter clothing in October and November, extra money for Christmas gifts, replacement of school clothing in the early spring, special clothing allowances for Easter, and graduation and summer camp clothing allowances for school children in May and June.

No MWRO affiliate won all of these benefits, but as long as it won *enough* victories to keep the organizers' promises credible, it seemed reasonable to believe that the members would keep coming back for more. "Benefit-of-the-month club" campaigns generally resembled the initial organizing drives. But the subsequent campaigns were also unlike the initial drives in that the organizers shared decisions about the timing and nature of the campaign with the local lay leadership, often lessening the efficiency with which the campaign was run.

The benefit-of-the-month club strategies did not, however, prove equal to the task of keeping local welfare rights affiliates alive. Repeated campaigns became disappointing to organizers, who had hoped to educate the membership to issues of political power, when they began to realize that members were interested only in tangible benefits. The typical organizer was concerned with justice; they cared only for bread.

As the benefit-of-the-month club became less attractive to MWRO organizers, other events reduced both the supply of such benefits and the demand for them. Welfare Department personnel became more experienced with confrontation tactics and developed negotiating skills that reduced the likelihood of outright capitulation. In addition, the growth of the MWRO prompted revisions in Massachusetts Welfare Department regulations that reduced the discretion of local welfare office directors to grant concessions to protest groups. Guidelines for requesting police assistance were issued and even more importantly freedom to accede to group demands was, in certain cases, made contingent upon approval of regional and state officials far from the scene of the disruption. For all of these reasons, it became increasingly difficult for a local welfare rights organization to continue intimidating the same welfare office with equal success.

These changes made it increasingly attractive for the group to attack new targets, but given the interests of local group membership, there appeared to be no other institution besides the Welfare Department that could provide the requisite benefits.

Repeated special needs campaigns also began to decrease in saliency to the veteran members. In the first place, satisfaction of a given need meant that the member had no further use for the organization unless another could be

activated to take its place. But the monetary value of later special needs campaigns could never equal that of the initial ones. Supplementary grants for furniture or household appliances might net a family hundreds of dollars, but grants
for school clothing could reach such levels only for exceptionally large families.
After these two campaigns, members could only be promised benefits worth a
few dollars a month, such as special diet allowances and replacement of worn
out school clothing. In addition, a considerable proportion of the general
membership undoubtedly learned how to win special needs grants for themselves.
Once the local group sent them a flyer announcing a benefit, they had no further
need to become involved in demonstrations.

The ultimate response by state welfare officials to greater recipient knowledge about special needs grants was implementation of a "flat grant" system
under which no supplementary checks would be issued. This change was adopted
in Massachusetts and a number of other states with active welfare rights affiliates
and has effectively eliminated the basic Boston model organizing tool in those
states.[a] But for the reasons cited above, most MWRO affiliates would not have
been able to maintain themselves even if the state had not adopted a flat grant.
In fact, most MWRO affiliates were moribund long before the institution of the
flat grant in that state.

Because of the shortcomings in the "benefit-of-the-month club" strategy,
MWRO organizers sought to supplement it with a variety of other techniques,
most of which were also tied to tangible impact on the lives of the members.
Dissemination of information about welfare rules and regulations was the most
efficient inducement available to the MWRO because there was little cost to the
organization in obtaining it, and it could often be relied upon to draw women
to meetings. Both the Massachusetts Welfare Department and the NWRO office
in Washington regularly sent the MWRO detailed information about changes in
welfare laws and administrative procedures that might affect members. The
Work Incentive Program (WIN) enacted in the 1967 amendments to the Social
Security law required certain categories of welfare recipients to take jobs or
training or else face the loss of their benefits. With the help of a major grant
from the Department of Labor, the NWRO printed and distributed thousands
of pamphlets describing the program and explaining how to get into it if one
were interested (and how to stay out if one were not)! The WIN program ran
into funding and administrative difficulties in Massachusetts and other states,
and there was little pressure on recipients to enter the program. But most recipients were unaware of this and were extremely anxious to learn how to avoid
being forced to go to work.

---

[a]The federal and state officials involved in the adoption of flat grant systems have
generally denied that special needs grants were adopted as a means of destroying welfare
rights organizations. In New York, the first state to adopt the flat grant, H.E.W. officials
stressed considerations of equity. As will be shown in Chapter 9, Massachusetts officials
were somewhat more candid.

In Massachusetts, pamphlets and other information were generally given only to MWRO members and only at local group meetings. The discussion of all new programs and procedures included ways to appeal unfavorable decisions and an offer of assistance any time this became necessary.

Some of the information given out at welfare rights meetings did not strictly fit under the rubric of learning one's rights under the law. At one local group meeting, for example, the chairman gave the following advice:

> *If you happen to get yourself a part-time job, you may have to fill out a form listing your Social Security number. If you get confused and write the last numbers as 4321 instead of 1234, the government may have a more difficult time keeping track of how much you are earning and how much they should therefore subtract from your welfare check. If you make a slip and say your name is May instead of Fay, the same thing might happen.*

Whether legal or not, such advice was quite helpful in saving members money. Informational meetings were also tied to benefit-to-the-month club campaigns. One meeting would be devoted to learning one's rights but the request forms would be withheld until a later meeting.

Although such uses of information proved useful in promoting attendance at meetings, they also had most of the drawbacks associated with special needs campaigns. Information—like tangible benefits—could be given to the same person only one time; once the member had it, she no longer needed the organization, and thus the organizers were still faced with a constant scramble to come up with new ideas. In addition to this, the welfare laws and practices did not change quickly enough to permit frequent meetings centered on these changes. Devoting two meetings to a single "benefit-of-the-month club" campaign violated the principle of minimum demand and experienced members quickly learned to distinguish between those meetings at which preliminary information would be given out and those meetings that would lead to demonstrations to "come and get it." Finally, extensive repetition of the same information for the benefit of new members of a group tended to bore veteran members, which increased the tendency for them to drop out and thus promoted high membership turnover even among the relatively more stable groups.

Other supplements to the "benefit-of-the-month club" strategy included techniques designed to associate regular attendance at meetings with additional tangible benefits. Along these lines, MWRO local groups promised their members that those with good attendance records would be rewarded with guaranteed credit of major department stores and with personalized assistance with grievances at the welfare offices.

A series of widely publicized agreements between the MWRO and several department and discount stores in Massachusetts were perhaps the single most effective inducement for continued membership participation in local affiliates.

There had been major debates within the welfare rights staff on both the
national and statewide levels over the desirability of luring welfare recipients
into agreements in which they would be paying 18 per cent annual interest
charges. Eventually the proponents of this course of action prevailed on the
strength of arguments ranging from the practical—"recipients pay much more
than 18 per cent when they borrow from less scrupulous sources"—to the more
straightforward—"the ladies want it." In the MWRO, the second argument had
considerably more weight, at least in the form that "the ladies want it and
therefore it provides an excellent (and obtainable) inducement to build and
maintain local groups." The MWRO staff did not, of course, put the argument
in precisely these terms, however.

The credit agreements in Massachusetts were achieved after a sophisticated
campaign that began with a MWRO announcement of support for the National
Welfare Rights Organization boycott and direct action campaign against Sears
Roebuck to win consumer credit. The NWRO had been encouraging its local
affiliates to participate in the "Sears campaign" by preparing thousands of
"how to do it" packets and spending several weeks engaged in telephone calls
to persuade local group organizers and leaders to join in the demand for credit.

Strictly speaking, the issue with Sears—and other stores as well—was not
a refusal on their part to give any credit to welfare recipients or even members
of the NWRO per se. What the stores claimed to be doing was to decide on the
merits of each application on an individual basis.[1] Welfare rights leaders retorted
that the usual decision in these cases was that the recipients' applications did
not meet the necessary standards; what they were demanding was an agreement
to give credit, under normal circumstances, to anyone bringing a letter of
recommendation signed by the leaders of their local welfare rights organization.
The leaders of welfare rights groups were careful to avoid any claim that they
would assume liability for the defaults of anyone whom they recommended.

The MWRO contribution to the nationwide credit campaign was a series
of "shop-ins" and a rather bizarre ceremony in which several non-recipient
supporters of the group burned their credit cards at the Cambridge Sears store
during the busy pre-Easter weeks of April, 1969. Although the buy-ins and
credit card burning were considered enjoyable by the participants, the only
change in Sears policy was the institution of a ban on demonstrations on store
property without prior permission of the store management.

The Cambridge Sears store was not the ultimate goal of the MWRO demonstrators, however. Instead the MWRO staff saw the demonstrations as an
opportunity to accumulate bargaining chips for negotiations with smaller
department store chains that could not absorb the same punishment as Sears.
Within a week of a Sears shop-in involving over 250 welfare mothers and
children, MWRO negotiators sought to discuss credit arrangements with a leading Massachusetts retail establishment. The manager replied that he could
not meet the MWRO demands without the cooperation of his major competitors.

Somewhat to their own surprise, the MWRO leaders soon found themselves in a series of meetings with the Boston Retail Trade Board and shortly after this, a series of credit agreements were signed with Boston's major department store chains—Jordan Marsh, Filene's, and Gilchrists.

The MWRO negotiators never made reference to their previous activities at Sear's but the memory of the sit-ins was undoubtedly fresh in everyone's minds and no further disruptive activity was necessary. Subsequent negotiations with Zayre discount store chain proved to be more difficult but an agreement was hastened by a few small scale demonstrations and the threats of still further action in the stores in Boston's black neighborhoods. This pattern of using Sears as a foil for other stores was repeated in other parts of the country as well. On the national level, a continuing "Sock it to Sears" campaign led to a limited credit agreement with Montgomery Ward. In New York City, the demonstrations against Sears were followed by credit agreements with such other major department stores as Gimbels, Abraham and Straus, and E.J. Korvettes.

Once the MWRO negotiating committee reached an agreement with the management of a store, they transferred the administration of the credit program to the lay leaders of the affiliated local groups. Local group chairmen were given complete autonomy in determining who should get the letters of recommendation, although the MWRO Executive Board strongly recommended that they be restricted to those who had attended three consecutive meetings and were up-to-date in their dues payments. Whenever this rule was adhered to, the lure of credit proved to be a major inducement to attract members to meetings where special needs grants were not involved.

However, the attempt to use credit letters as a means of organizational maintenance proved unequal to the task, as had most other MWRO methods. Once credit letters were granted, those receiving them had no further need to participate in local group activities, and the organizers were faced with the familiar problem of coming up with something new. Development of this problem was often hastened by the local group chairmen who were often freer in distributing credit letters than their organizers preferred. Many letters were given to those with only sporadic attendance records which negated the major intended purpose.

Conversations between members of the MWRO staff and other organizers led to the idea of consumer credit at stores that would give discounts to active members of local group affiliates. It had been pointed out that groups that could promise a significant number of discounts could charge considerable monthly dues and eventually reach financial independence. However, MWRO affiliates in Boston and Springfield that tried this strategy were not successful in their negotiations with the stores; they were unable to counter storeowners' arguments about tiny profit margins. (Some MWRO organizers successfully adopted this tactic in later community organizing activities, however.)

A second major benefit-related service offered by welfare rights groups was known as "grievance work," which was assistance with individual problems. It is impossible to characterize all the kinds of grievances that welfare recipients held against their caseworkers, but the more usual ones included failure to receive a regular welfare check, failure to receive an emergency food order or a special needs grant, attempts to deduct emergency payments from subsequent checks, failure of a caseworker to show proper respect, excessive prying by caseworkers, or inability to reach a caseworker when necessary.

In theory, the grievance settling procedures of MWRO local groups were complex. Members of local groups were given the opportunity to volunteer for a grievance committee and thereby serve as a voting member of the local group executive board. Grievance committee members were trained in the intricacies of welfare law and how best to motivate (or intimidate) caseworkers into changing their minds. Local group members with problems would then be referred to a member of the grievance committee who would first discuss the problem and then offer to accompany the member to the welfare office to serve as an advocate.

In reality, however, there were rarely more than one or two members of a local group with both the ability and the willingness to serve as effective advocates for others. Most often these were the chairman and perhaps another elected officer; grievance committee members, who devoted a good deal of time to the organization, generally preferred an elective office and used their work on the committee as a means to gain that end. MWRO organizers rarely did grievance work for members although they sometimes made exceptions for especially active—and hence valuable members of the group—or for members who had developed personal animosities with the grievance workers for their groups. In complex cases, local group grievance workers would call the MWRO statewide office to get an opinion from a staff lawyer or experienced organizer. Members calling the statewide office directly, however, were referred back to the chairman of their local groups.

When MWRO grievance workers came across cases in which the prospects of success were particularly dim, they invited the member to accompany them to the next demonstration at her welfare office. In the heat of welfare office confrontations, many members proved to be more willing to help their fellow members than one would have guessed from their previous behavior. In part, they may have realized that they too might be involved in a similar situation in the future and would like others to pitch in and help them. But for the most part, the decisions to stay and fight for others after one's own demands were met appeared to represent a feeling of "community" emerging in demonstrations. In the heat of the confrontation situation, a high proportion of recipients appeared to derive satisfaction from declaring their solidarity with others involved in heated struggle with "the common enemy" and from seeing caseworkers backing down regardless of whether they personally gained tangible benefits or not.

In part, the solidarity that developed in demonstrations can be traced to efforts to nurture it by the MWRO organizers who were present. But it can not be completely attributed to the influence of non-recipients with different value systems. Local group organizers were at times overruled by their members when they advised that a single person's problem was not worth the risk of everyone getting arrested. In one example, the members of the group voted to continue a sit-in beyond the normal welfare office closing time simply because one of their members did not receive a ten-dollar food order. The organizer, feeling highly satisfied with the successful special needs benefit campaign already completed, was unwilling to take a chance in having the day end in arrests for the sake of ten dollars for one member but felt compelled to abide by the vote of members. In that case, the organizer and his group got off the hook as the harried welfare office director personally approved the food order request and the group was allowed to leave peaceably with a total victory.

In those states in which a flat grant system has been instituted to eliminate the provision for special needs grants, welfare rights organizers have had to give a higher priority to the settlement of individual grievances. In New York City, for example, the major focus for welfare rights demonstrations has been grievance work. There have, however, been efforts at providing a common theme to demonstrations by looking at broad areas in which all or most members might share grievances. Some New York City demonstrations have thus been directed towards forcing a review of the basic budgetary allowance for each member of the group to make sure she was getting everything to which she was entitled.

Reliance upon grievance work as an inducement to elicit continued membership participation had many of the same limitations as did the lure of tangible benefits or information. Only a small fraction of the membership could be depended upon to have pressing grievances at any given meeting time, and many of those who did were unwilling to wait until they had demonstrated commitment to the group before seeking assistance. The effectiveness of grievance work in promoting participation was further weakened as veteran members discovered they could get assistance with their problems regardless of their status as an active contributor to the group.

The basic problem with grievance work, however, was that a settled grievance, like other fulfilled needs, left no further incentive to contribute to the group. The interests of the MWRO staff in seeking to create a stronger organization were constantly thwarted by the unending need to devise new ways to prove the usefulness of welfare rights; they had to run faster and faster merely to stay in place.

In all of the techniques for group maintenance heretofore discussed, the MWRO affiliates sought to prompt continued participation by offering certain benefits, information, or services only to those who make continued contributions to organization activities. These dispassionate attempts to link benefits

to participation often led to conflict between the MWRO organizers and lay
leaders. Many local group lay leaders refused to neglect needy fellow welfare
recipients who had not actively participated in welfare rights activities. Unless
under the careful eye of organizers, they offered to help anyone who came to
them with a grievance problem or gave special needs request forms to those
who merely promised to join or participate actively in the future.

In a few cases, MWRO affiliates seeking additional program material
departed from the benefits-for-members-only paradign to press for benefits
available to the entire community or at least the low-income segment of the
community. Some MWRO affiliates worked to keep surplus food offices open
for longer periods of time and to force the local public housing authority
management to improve maintenance of apartments and grounds. In two
cases, MWRO affiliates pressed local school committees to gain free or reduced
price school lunches for all low-income families. MWRO organizers discussed—
but never implemented—a "utilities campaign" to demand lower rates or smaller
deposits for low-income individuals.

Many MWRO organizers viewed the surplus food, housing conditions, school
lunch, and utilities campaigns as having a great potential for transforming local
welfare rights affiliates into multi-issue groups, which would broaden the movement's base and expand its constituency from welfare recipients to all poor
people. Others looked to these activities to build alliances with other community
groups. None appeared to elicit much interest from the MWRO general membership, however, and none were attempted by more than one or two local groups.
Only the school lunch campaign brought the unambiguous victories that the
MWRO staff held to be vital to group maintenance, and despite the enthusiasm
created among the organizers, none ever came close to fulfilling its potential.

Limitations of Other Strategies

Despite their ingenuity, the MWRO staff and leadership were unable to tie
all meetings and other organizational activities to the receipt of sizeable, tangible personal gains, or even information about such gains. For this reason,
they also sought to provide side benefits or intangible rewards, while further
reducing the demands placed on members.

It was most difficult to provide sizeable tangible benefits at those activities
designed solely to carry out organizational business such as the MWRO annual
membership conventions or such ceremonial occasions as the June 30, 1969,
"birthday of the movement" rally.

Conceivably these activities could have been linked with special needs grants
campaigns, following the business meetings with confrontations at welfare offices.
This was not attempted for a number of reasons. In part this was because of the
logistical problems in getting members back to their *local* welfare offices, the
only source of benefits. But perhaps more important than this was a desire to

project a favorable image in the press, showing that the MWRO was as able to carry out peaceful mass meetings as were other groups.

The agenda at the conventions consisted almost exclusively of self-congratulatory speeches and the election of statewide officers. The conventions attractiveness therefore derived from maximizing side benefits and minimizing demand. In doing this, the staff arranged for free transportation, free lunches for the membership, and free baby-sitting service. Unsuccessful efforts were made to get "name" entertainment to perform at the conventions and to get Senator Edward Kennedy to speak—not so much to attract the press as to attract the recipient membership.

Similarly, the chief inducements to attend the June 30 birthday rally were free transportation, a personal appearance by George Wiley (who was a much greater draw for the membership than was "featured speaker" Dr. Benjamin Spock), and a picnic-like atmosphere complete with free helium balloons for the children.

There were, however, drawbacks to the use of such inducements. Many were financial; providing free meals, transportation, and even several thousand helium balloons was not a burden the MWRO could transfer to the Welfare Department as was the case with special needs grants. Providing this type of incentive, therefore, served as a major drain upon the group and its limited resources. Babysitting would also have incurred huge costs had it not been provided by the MWRO staff.

A less obvious, but by no means unimportant, factor involved in continued participation of the general membership was the attraction of meeting friends (or potential friends) or at least fighting loneliness and boredom. The relative importance of these motives was difficult to measure and undoubtedly varied from member to member and group to group, but a very large percentage of those contacted by MWRO doorknocking teams did appear to be relatively isolated. Few had participated in organized group activities since leaving school, and most limited their social contacts to a small number of close friends or relatives. In many housing projects, the majority of those contacted did not seem to know neighbors who lived on the same floor. A high proportion of these people appeared to be anxious to "get out of the house" and get involved with others once their initial suspicion and hostility were overcome.

The friendship motive appeared to be more important in isolated communities or those with a smaller proportion of welfare recipients. On Cape Cod, a local group had about 50 members, almost of whom were either related or close friends. Their monthly meetings were great social occasions at which refreshments, including liquor, were shared. Members arrived long before meetings were scheduled to begin and stayed until the meeting room was locked for the night. The members of this group were not only geographically isolated but ethnically distinctive as well; belonging to the local group played a major role uniting them. Similarly, a welfare rights affiliate in a small town in western Massachusetts enrolled 35 of 37 eligible recipients and managed to continue functioning without much assistance from the MWRO staff or much emphasis on Boston model organizing drives.

The class background of the members and surrounding community also played a role in determining the extent to which social motives would predominate. White, middle-class affiliates of the MWRO often took on some of the characteristics of suburban voluntary organizations. One group chose to supplement its grievance committee with a refreshment committee and an entertainment committee.

The friendship factor was not apparent in the *initial* meetings of the larger welfare rights groups based in the Boston and Springfield housing projects. As the groups dwindled in size, however an increasing proportion of the remaining members appeared more socially inclined, which might have been a result of their feeling more at ease in smaller groups or, more generally, the fact that those who best responded to solidary incentives had remained active. But in any event, these incentives played an increasing role in the continued participation of those who remained active after the majority of members lapsed into inactivity. Thus, groups that were most isolated, both from the wider community and from the MWRO central staff's emphasis on tangible rewards and the Boston model "benefit-of-the-month club" campaigns, were most likely to remain active over a long period.

While the friendship and social motives did not create a financial drain on welfare rights affiliates, reliance upon them had other costs. In the first place, they were usually insufficient for attracting more than a handful of members. For those members who were getting together primarily to have a good time, there was little reason to engage in such potentially troublesome activities as demonstrations that carried the risk of arrest. Similarly, those who were primarily motivated by friendship or a desire to end boredom were less likely to view the maldistribution of influence in society as the cause of their problems and were therefore less responsive to the MWRO organizers' stress on building the power of the poor to rectify things.

The welfare rights movement did try to promote a sense of solidarity and unity among welfare recipients throughout the country by distributing the NWRO newspaper to all local affiliates. This newspaper might have contributed to local group maintenance by continually emphasizing successful accomplishments of other affiliates. There is little evidence however that either the NWRO newspaper or its Massachusetts counterpart, "The Adequate Income Times," positively affected the general membership.

The Impact of Maintenance Needs on
MWRO Operating Style

All things being equal, one might have expected that MWRO to rely heavily on mass rallies in Boston. After the state takeover of welfare in 1968, all major decisions on welfare policy were made in that city. The massing of hundreds if not thousands of welfare recipients from all parts of the state would have provided graphic stories for the mass media, which would have helped further the image of a powerful broad-based organization. The presence of recipients from so many different groups in a single location would also have enhanced the concept of statewide organization for the general membership and given them visible proof of their numbers if not their power. Finally, adherance to the Boston model principle that numbers equals power should have dictated a smaller number of large demonstrations rather than the reverse.

As it was, however, typical MWRO action comprised simultaneous local group demonstrations that divided the members into relatively small groups and kept the full fury of the movement from the Boston welfare administrators, from the media, and perhaps most importantly of all, from the members themselves.

Small group activities were necessitated in part, by the logistical difficulties and financial strain involved in transporting large numbers of people from all parts of a state the size of Massachusetts to any single point. But some means of handling both logistics and finances might have been developed were it not for the principle that welfare rights organizers should ask as little of the membership as possible. In this regard, there was no comparison between a strategy that required a two- or three-hour morning walk for few blocks to fill out a form and receive an immediate monetary reward and the alternative that required volunteering for an activity that would take up an entire day, necessitate making babysitting and lunch arrangements, and sitting on a bus for long hours in the hope that the action would result in some betterment in the indeterminate future. For an organization meticulous enough to collect membership dues only directly after "check day" in order to minimize demand, the single mass rally was just too much of a violation of that principle to be employed except on rare occasions.

Even if recipients might have been convinced to make all the sacrifices for a day trip to Boston, the only place they could ultimately get special needs grants was in their local welfare offices. A single mass rally followed by a mass dispersal to various local welfare offices would have been, in effect, two demonstrations for a single benefit, which constituted violation of the principle of minimum demand.

The MWRO did engage in a number of demonstrations that brought together representatives of most of its affiliates, but for the reasons outlined above, these were generally limited in size and rarely exceeded 100 or 150 participants. Most of those present at the statewide demonstrations were members of the local groups closest to the action or perhaps a more recently formed group from further away. The outlying groups were usually represented by small delegations—often only an activist coterie of 5 or less. The small statewide demonstrations that took place outside of Boston, site of the greatest concentration of welfare rights members in the state, or Springfield, site of the second largest concentration, were usually attended by only the activists without any general membership phalanx to provide the numbers. Two MWRO statewide demonstrations aimed at harassing the Massachusetts governor when he spoke in Worcester and Waltham thus involved only about two dozen members, leaders, and staff.

The inability of the MWRO to assemble more than a fraction of its membership in any single location did not put the organization to as much of a disadvantage as might be thought, however. In the first place, much of the negotiating with government officials could be carried out by only small committees of MWRO lay leaders. Although these lay leaders needed some organizational activity to maintain their legitimacy, this activity was just as easily maintained by coordinated local demonstrations as by larger mass demonstrations. In fact, they were often able to strengthen a case by being able to point to a series of demonstrations across the state. As will be argued in Chapter 9, this same process of legitimization through widely scattered demonstrations by local and state welfare rights organizations was used by George Wiley and the NWRO lay leaders to justify their representing American welfare recipients when they appeared before Congress and administrative agencies.

The MWRO's limited capacity to mobilize large numbers for statewide demonstrations can also be seen as less of a barrier to the attainment of organizational goals when one distinguishes between two basic styles of protest. The Boston model style of protest involved only two parties, a protest group that approached a target and offered the following bargain: if you concede to my demands, I will stop disrupting your office, which you undoubtedly find more unpalatable than the concessions I ask. The premises of the Boston model were appropriate for this sort of demonstration because increased numbers (up to a certain point) did lead to increased disruption and hence increased coercive potential.

The MWRO statewide demonstrations were not, for the most part, intended to be coercive; the MWRO was not in a position to coerce the state legislature or governor into giving concessions. Symbolic actions designed to increase the visibility of the organization and to bolster its reputation were used to minimize future need for employing disruptive activities or to clarify its stand on various issues. The messages the MWRO sought to convey were often intended for audiences who were not physically present but would be reached through the mass media. In these instances, absolute numbers involved in a demonstration were less important than the modest-sized turnout required to attract the attention of the media and the perception that the demonstrators could legitimately speak for others who were similarly situated but not physically present. The statewide demonstrations with the greatest turnout, the June 30th birthday rally and the two annual conventions were primarily directed toward gaining publicity and serving internal organizational purposes. These styles of protest

resemble the paradigms presented by James Q. Wilson[2] and Michael Lipsky[3]
respectively. A discussion of the paradigms and how they fit into a broader
theory of protest is contained in Chapter 8.

A Fundamental Problem: Conflict between Staff and Leaders

The discussion to this point has focused primarily upon two basic components of the welfare rights movement: the organizing staff seeking to form local
groups to build the power of the poor, and the general membership acting to
maximize the receipt of tangible benefits. While these two forms of motivation
coincided during the Boston model organizing drives described in Chapter 3,
they separated after the first few demonstrations by each new MWRO affiliate.

The problems created by these disparate goals were complicated by the
development of a third point of view on the part of the MWRO lay leadership.
In retrospect, the conflicts between the staff, who were looking toward change,
growth, and new directions, and the MWRO lay leaders, who tended to question
the need for change, appeared to destroy any possibility of instituting basic
modifications in the Boston model in order to help solve the problem of local
group maintenance.

The first step in the direction of conflict was the development by the MWRO
lay leaders of the perception that they were as important to the staff as the staff
was to them. With the passage of time, MWRO leaders on both the local group
and statewide level saw that without them, organizers would have no legitimacy.
Many began making demands upon their organizers in return for the support
that had been uncritically given in the past. Those leaders who did not develop
this awareness on their own were quickly informed at the MWRO statewide
meetings by their counterparts in other groups. Once this level of consciousness
had been achieved, the question of who was influencing whom in the movement
became virtually impossible to answer.

On the statewide level, the MWRO Executive Board questioned whether
the division of power between themselves and the organizers that was favored
by the staff was necessarily the best one. The history of the MWRO was marked
by repeated attempts by the MWRO Executive Board to increase its decision-
making power at the expense of the staff. Many of these attempts were successful. One area of major concern to the lay leaders was the organization of new
local affiliates. Originally, every detail of the Boston model drive described in
Chapter 3 was in the hands of the staff. With the passage of time, the MWRO
Executive Board involved itself with the issue of which areas should be organized
and in the running of the first meetings. In part these accretions of power
resulted from the belief of the Executive Board that it should play a larger role
in running the organization, but their heightened interest can also be attributed

to the desire to increase their visibility to local group members and to build personal ties with the new local group leaders. Both of these desires were derived from their increasing preoccupation with re-election. To the extent that the MWRO lay leaders were unaware or unconcerned with the subtleties of the Boston model—such as never using the word "demonstration"—the MWRO first meetings and first confrontations were more difficult to run and the job of the organizers became more complex.

The MWRO staff pressed for a provision in the statewide organization's bylaws that voting strength for each local group at the annual conventions would be proportional to the number of dues-paying members it had in the hope that this would give all lay leaders seeking higher office an incentive to build their membership. Unfortunately, once that higher office had been attained, and until just before the next convention, there was little reason for most lay leaders to pay much attention to maintaining or expanding their groups. Some lay leaders opposed staff efforts to revitalize their groups partly because of their fear that the new membership faction might hold potential challengers to the incumbent's chairmanship. At times, leaders of a dwindling group agreed to new organizing drives but stipulated that no new local elections be held. In such cases, stalemates occurred; the MWRO staff refused to help recruit new members under those conditions.

Another conflict between organizers and lay leaders concerned the issue of secondary leadership for local groups. The MWRO staff members sought to nurture the development of as many leaders within each local group as possible and to promote the division of responsibility among as many women as they could induce to play an active role. This policy was considered desirable in terms of increasing group effectiveness in confrontations, insuring internal democracy, and providing for easy leadership succession within the local groups. It was also considered worthy for its own sake—that is, such a plan helped members develop their abilities. However, local group chairman often saw these activities as efforts to undermine their leadership. As they became jealous about the roles played by others, local group chairmen began opposing delegation of tasks to potential rivals. Since few chairmen were willing to devote all the time necessary to perform all these tasks themselves, important things were left undone and the local groups deteriorated further.

Perhaps the worst problem involving such centralized leadership was that of replacing someone who held a monopoly of knowledge on how to run a group. Except in those cases when a lay leader was succeeded by a close friend or a chosen successor, the election of a new chairman usually meant the intro-duction of a whole new leadership clique in the group; in many ways it repre-sented starting from scratch once again.

Opposition to staff plans for major new organizing drives in those sections of Boston's black ghetto that had not yet been organized was expressed by the predominantly black MWRO leadership who, in part, feared the creation of new centers of power in the organization. In one case, such a drive took place only because the MWRO Executive Board felt sure that those who would be elected leaders of the new group would respect their seniority. In another, the worst fears of the Executive Board were realized when the chairman of a newer black group in Roxbury challenged and defeated the incumbent MWRO statewide chairman at the 1970 MWRO convention.

Perhaps the final phase in the developing rifts between lay leaders and staff came when some local lay leaders began to realize that they did not need strong groups to play an important role in MWRO statewide politics, and the MWRO Executive Board began to reach the parallel conclusion that the honors and respect they were receiving from politicians, welfare administrators, and leaders in the social welfare community did not really require a functioning statewide grassroots organization at all.

The conflict of interest between the maintenance of a militant protest organization based on disruption and the inclusion of its leadership on advisory or policy-making bodies that require "responsible" conduct is an obvious one, and we shall therefore confine ourselves to a single example of how it affected the MWRO. The Massachusetts Conference on Social Welfare, a private, social work-oriented organization, made it a practice to select the chairman of the MWRO to serve on its Board of Directors. When the governor of Massachusetts decided to institute a "flat grant" welfare system, he chose a meeting of the MCSW as the forum to make his announcement. The chairman of the MWRO chose to sit on stage near the podium from which the governor spoke rather than lead a group of her members to that podium to disrupt the speech. Her presence on stage effectively blunted the possibility of a militant protest on that occasion. Although the MWRO staff repeatedly warned the lay leaders about the dangers of cooptation, the MWRO Executive Board (like the MAW leaders before them) proved less wary of the dangers and more willing to take their chances.

For all these reasons, the disagreements between MWRO organizers and their lay leaders grew at an accelerating pace throughout the history of the organization. What began as minor differences of opinion sometimes escalated into personal animosities. Some MWRO local group organizers sought to deal with increasingly assertive veteran leaders by abandoning their groups to work on other drives or in the MWRO statewide office in an administrative position. When veteran lay leaders sought to further demonstrate their control over the staff by setting requirements for the original organizer's replacement—"I want only female organizers"— the MWRO staff director often proved unable or unwilling to meet the requirements and left the job unfilled. In some cases this represented a deliberate decision to let the group further deteriorate and weaken the influence of the assertive leader within the organization. This tactic never proved successful, however, since a lay leader's reputation long outlasted her ability to deliver any members to statewide demonstrations.

The organizers who remained with their local groups were often forced to choose between carrying out the wishes of their local group chairman and taking actions they felt were necessary for the future development and growth of those groups and the statewide organization. They usually chose to do the latter, which thus subverted the wishes of the leaders they opposed.

Although the willingness to intervene in local group politics varied among MWRO organizers, most eventually adopted the position that if a lay leader refused to be reasoned with, the organizer had a responsibility to help in the selection of leaders who would insure the future growth of the group. A number of MWRO staff members became involved in activities to bring about the resignation or electoral defeat of recalcitrant (from their point of view) leaders.

The most obvious case of a MWRO staff member refusing to accede to the wishes of the lay leadership was Bill Pastreich's refusal to accept the November 1969 decision of the MWRO Statewide Executive Board to postpone the upcoming elections and unilaterally extend its own term of office. Pastreich's decision to play the role of "guardian of the group's constitution" rather than "servant of the lay leadership" led to a bitterness that persisted throughout the history of the organization.

The major cleavage within the MWRO in the months following the February, 1970 statewide convention was a direct outgrowth of this dispute. The victorious slate at that convention was put together with the assistance of a few members of the MWRO staff and was headed by leaders of more recently organized local groups who were relatively receptive and responsive to the wishes of the MWRO staff. The defeated slate was centered around the oldest MWRO affiliates whose veteran leaders had developed their own independent set of priorities for the group and had therefore sought to foil the organizers by postponing the elections.

When the defeated incumbent chairman refused to recognize the validity of the election, only the intervention and mediation of NWRO staff and lay leaders prevented the total dissolution of the MWRO. As it was, the welfare rights movement in Massachusetts never recovered the momentum lost during the months of internal dissension.

Had the MWRO staff acquiesced to the desires of the lay leadership and postponed the convention and election, it would have foreclosed any immediate possibility of the organization evolving along the lines set out by Pastreich and his followers. Instead it would, in all probability, have led to the statewide organization dying the same slow death experienced by most of its local affiliates.

On the other hand, outright opposition to the wishes of the lay leadership was a clearcut invocation of the superiority of the organizers' values over those of the elected leaders. This decision led to a good deal of acrimony between staff and leaders. Had the leadership elected in February of 1970 been allowed to prevail, the close ties between staff and lay leaders, upon which the Boston model depended, might have been restored, and the organization would have sought new directions in an effort to save itself. As it was, the ousted leadership was eventually restored to office, which removed any immediate possibility of fruitful interaction with the existing staff but at least held the possibility that cooperation might be restored at some time in the future.

In reviewing this history of conflict between organizers and lay leaders, the question arises why the latter did not seek to dismiss the former—or at least the staff director—and seek more pliant successors or perhaps no successor at all. Welfare rights lay leaders from other parts of the country often spoke of firing all non-welfare recipient staff but their MWRO colleagues almost always stood up for "their" staff.

In part this was because the MWRO lay leaders had internalized the underlying principle of the Boston model that non-recipient organizers are necessary for the preservation of their groups. Local groups were especially dependent upon their organizers in fund-raising activities. Local group fund-raising events such as dances, cake sales, or "soul food dinners" required considerable time and effort. Local group leaders who were not used to such exertion and who found that their membership weaned on the principle of minimum demand were reluctant to participate in the planning. For this reason, few local groups could plan and execute enough fund-raising activities to support their own organizer, and once the organizer brought his own funding with him, it was difficult for the local group leaders to control what he did.

Almost every source of local group funds was tapped through the efforts of organizers. MWRO simplified welfare manuals that were given to local groups to sell, a television set to be raffled off (each group kept the proceeds for its own treasury), and proposals for funding from church groups and antipoverty groups were all obtained or prepared with only minimal participation of lay leaders. The funds raised by the MWRO were sent to the National Welfare Rights Organization's Washington headquarters for safekeeping (or loan to other affiliates) and only a few organizers fully understood the bookkeeping system that determined how much of that money could be drawn upon at any given time. It was therefore inconceivable to most MWRO lay leaders during most of organization history that they could get along on their own or that other organizers would be any better than the ones they then had.

This discussion of the conflicts between organizers and lay leaders brings us back to the preliminary explanation for the inability of MWRO affiliates to maintain themselves presented at the beginning of this chapter. Close cooperation between organizers and leaders was necessary—although not sufficient—to the flourishing of these local groups. It is conceivable that with continued cooperation the organizers and leaders together might have devised ways of dealing with the dilemmas outlined in the remainder of the chapter and developed the needed modifications of the Boston model.

As it was, however, that cooperation could not be maintained, and the key issue to be resolved is whether the conflict between organizers and leaders

was an accident of personality, whether it was the inevitable result of organizer—lay leader differences, or whether it resulted from any weaknesses within
the Boston model that had defined the initial relationships between organizer
and lay leader. The acrimony between organizers and lay leaders within the
welfare rights movement at all levels and in many locations throughout the
country appear to rule out both the first and the third possibilities. The answer
thus appears to lie in the general organizer—lay leader relationships common to
all welfare rights groups whether or not they adopted the Boston model. The
isolation of the precise problem areas in that relationship and the development
of a model that can resolve these problems would appear to be a necessary—
though again not necessarily sufficient—condition for the resolution of the
difficulties discussed in this chapter.

5 MWRO Staff

Organization does not come out of an immaculate conception. It takes a highly trained, politically sophisticated, creative organizer to do the job.

—Saul Alinsky[1]

The MWRO staff was the dominant component in the welfare rights movement in Massachusetts. Organizing drives were dependent upon the presence of MWRO staff for direction, as a major input on the doorknocking teams, and during the first meetings and confrontations. The difficulties encountered in maintaining the local groups that emerged from those organizing drives resulted in large part from staff attitudes towards community organization and in particular the staff preference for activities that gave them tangible evidence of their effectiveness.

The most distinctive feature of the MWRO staff was its size and its elaborate structure which encompassed a number of differentiated roles and functions. Typically, the National Welfare Rights Organization had only one or two full-time organizers in major United States cities and states. In Massachusetts, there was a goal of one organizer for each local group, which both permitted a considerably greater staff input than in other localities and at the same time created a major financial burden upon the organization. Within a two-year span after the first NWRO organizer came to the state, the MWRO employed 57 individuals as more or less full-time staff members and an even greater number as part-time staff or volunteers.

Because the Boston model was dependent upon a large staff, and because the National Welfare Rights Organization could never afford to pay the salaries of more than three MWRO staff members at any one time (and frequently less), the achievements of the MWRO must be attributed in large part to the ability of Bill Pastreich and his followers for discovering sympathetic individuals who had the ability to provide staff services. Additional sources of MWRO staff funding ranged from VISTA officials who were willing to allow VISTA volunteers to be assigned to welfare rights groups (and other VISTA officials who were misled as to the true nature of their volunteers' activities) to social work professors who were willing to grant field placements for their students to work for welfare rights. In addition to this, other academic, social welfare, and antipoverty

77

organizations sometimes allocated funds to support MWRO staff. Proposals submitted to foundations and church groups accounted for the bulk of the remaining funds used to support MWRO organizers.

But despite this wide variety, the VISTA program was by far the largest
single source of support for MWRO staff. A substantial majority of those who
worked for the MWRO in its first year of existence were supported for at least
several months by the VISTA program. This dependence upon VISTAs was not
unique to the MWRO. Two writers close to the welfare rights movement have
written that over 200 VISTAs had worked for the NWRO as its "chief organizing
resource."[2]

The constraints imposed upon protest group activity by dependence upon
outsiders for funding are well recognized. (Cesar Chavez is reported to have
rejected the offer of a $50,000 grant with no conditions attached whatsoever
because he felt that even this sort of contribution would put pressure upon him
to obtain immediate results.[3]) The welfare rights movement has shown an
amazing disregard for these constraints by refusing to allow direct grants from
the federal government to inhibit sit-ins in government offices and refusing to
let the knowledge that a VISTA volunteer arrested in a demonstration might be
released from the program inhibit the activities of VISTAs. The ability of
others to replicate the experience of the MWRO thus appears to be dependent
upon their ability to find similar sources of support and avoid the constraints.
Although academic and social welfare support can, in all probability, still be
found in at least some of the major urban centers, the continuing withdrawal
of the VISTA programs from large cities and from community organization
activities make it unlikely that such a high level of outside support as experienced by the MWRO can be obtained in the near future.

The size of the MWRO staff permitted a degree of functional specializa-
tion far beyond the capacity of most other welfare rights groups. At first
all MWRO organizers did virtually the same thing, but within a few months
of the first organizing drives, four distinct roles emerged. The first was the
"inner circle," the principal organizer (also known as the staff director) who
had final say over all decisions to be made, and his chief lieutenants. These
were generally the members of the staff with the most seniority and experience,
but the crucial factor in their selection was the confidence which the chief
organizer had in their judgment. Only 8 of the 57 MWRO staff members ever
were a part of this inner circle.

Most MWRO staff members were local group organizers, assigned to one
or two local MWRO affiliates. Their role in decision-making at the statewide
level was usually limited to giving specific information about these groups and
estimating how they would react to a given course of action. Virtually all
MWRO staff members played this role when they first joined the organization;
over half never played any other.

Two other functions were performed by specialized groups of staff members.

Four organizers restricted themselves almost entirely to secretarial duties and four others carried out what was known as "middle-class work"—negotiating with politicians, officials of the Welfare Department, voluntary social welfare organizations, the mass media, and other individuals or organizations that might make financial contributions to the movement.

There were four distinct periods in the development of the MWRO staff: a founding period roughly coinciding with the 1968–69 academic year in which the staff slowly grew to roughly one dozen; a period of rapid organizational growth in the summer of 1969 in which the staff increased to several dozen; a period of consolidation in the academic year 1969–70 in which the number of organizers slowly diminished; and an intensified search for new directions beginning in the late spring and early summer of 1970 during which the size of the staff continued to dwindle. There were few differences among those staff members entering in the four periods, although as we have already indicated, the new arrivals were always disproportionately represented in the role of local group organizer while the old-timers were far more likely to be members of the inner circle.

The Composition of the MWRO Staff

The typical MWRO staff member was a white, middle-class, recent college graduate. The staff was roughly evenly divided between men and women although the inner circle included only men and the local group organizers were mostly women. These factors had important implications for Boston model organizing drives and in shaping the inner dynamics of the organization.

For a number of years, writers have noted the rise in racial consciousness and concluded that ghetto blacks could only be organized by other blacks. The whites remaining on the Student Nonviolent Coordinating Committee staff after May 1966 were asked to confine their efforts to organizing poor whites.[4] A study of the Congress of Racial Equality notes that although Floyd McKissick denied that the group's shift from non-violent direct action towards organizing the ghettos meant the exclusion of whites from the organization, "the move toward ghetto organization moves naturally in that direction."[5] Saul Alinsky, whose thinking was instrumental in determining the attitudes of the MWRO staff took the same position:

> "I accept the fact that today, in spite of my record, my white skin disqualified me from the kind of direct organizing work I've done in Chicago and Rochester. . . . In this climate I'm convinced that all whites should get out of black ghettos."[6]

The welfare rights movement explicitly rejected any emphasis on "black power" in favor of an emphasis on "poor people's power" and gave prominence to its poor white, Spanish-speaking and Indian members. But the bulk of the membership of the National Welfare Rights Organization has always come from precisely those ghetto areas that experts in community organization are increasingly describing as off-limits to whites. Although the MWRO had probably organized a higher proportion of white welfare recipients than any other statewide welfare rights affiliate, the question remains as to how the predominantly white staff of the MWRO could have succeeded in implementing the Boston model regardless of the racial background of those they were organizing.

Before explaining the MWRO ability to organize blacks with a virtually all-white staff, it should be noted that Bill Pastreich would have preferred to have more black organizers but found it difficult to recruit them. In the first place, educated and talented young blacks found they could get considerably higher salaries for considerably less grueling work in fields other than community organizing. Secondly, the MWRO's rejection of the expressive goals such as "black power" served to put the organization at a disadvantage compared to campus-based black student unions. Black organizers who were dividing their time between the MWRO and campus-based black organizations soon left the welfare rights movement for those other groups. The one black who remained with the staff the longest felt that "increasing black political consciousness" should have been added to the usually discussed organizational priorities.[7]

These considerations account for the limited number of black welfare rights organizers in Massachusetts (and throughout the country for that matter), but they do not explain how in the face of the rising black consciousness in the ghettos, the MWRO was able to build a strong organization with a predominantly white staff. How in particular was the MWRO able to serve as the major spokesman for hundreds of ghetto blacks for nearly a year before it was able to recruit its first full-time black staff member?

Part of the answer lies in the sharp distinction that the MWRO staff always drew between themselves and recipient members of the affiliated welfare rights organizations—that is, between organizers and "the ladies" as they were called. MWRO staff members were always careful to see that the recipients received all public credit for what was accomplished; lay leaders were encouraged ro run all MWRO meetings, to lead demonstrations and marches, and to engage in negotiations for themselves while their organizers remained in the background. MWRO staff never made statements to the press; only lay leaders and members were permitted to do so.

Because of this, the black lay leadership were less inclined to perceive white organizers as personal threats; instead they saw them as assistants to help maintain their own positions of public prominence. Black lay leaders of the MWRO often defended "their" organizers to the black leadership of other community organizations. The fact that the organizers were white made it difficult to assume a direct leadership role even had they wanted to, but in general, the issue of whites leading a black organization did not arise because the white took pains not to be leaders (or at least not to appear to be leaders).

Even more basically, the ability of the MWRO to organize blacks with a predominantly white staff was derived—as was so much else—from the organization's proven effectiveness to win victories that made a tangible difference in the lives of the membership. Once the issue was seen in terms of a realistic chance to win such benefits, the overwhelming majority of MWRO members were concerned only with who could best deliver those goods, not with the color of his skin.

As long as the white organizers were able to "deliver" material benefits, the MWRO membership never raised the issue of race. This concern with an individual's effectiveness rather than his background may also explain the decision by a number of white welfare rights affiliates to elect one of the few blacks in their membership to the lay leadership, presumably, because a black might be more intimidating in welfare office confrontations.

The experience of the MWRO thus suggests that it is still possible for whites to play an active role in creating black organizations—if they can deliver the goods. But this statement requires several qualifications. In the first place, the acceptance of white, middle-class organizers by lower-class blacks in Boston between 1968 and 1970 does not mean that all blacks in all circumstances would be willing to do so. It is conceivable that in the future, values such as race pride will acquire increased relevance for large numbers of poor, minority group members, so that they will be willing to forego any benefits not offered by members of their own race or ethnic background. Indigenous ghetto leaders may also begin to learn the skills that had previously been monopolized by white organizers and thus be in a stronger position to force whites out of the ghetto and to provide the benefits themselves.

The second qualification applies to the organizer's tasks that go beyond direct contact with the general membership. White organizers remain severely handicapped in representing their black constituents at conferences and meetings of other predominantly black organizations. White organizers are also less effective than blacks in fund-raising with white liberals and in press relations. More broadly, as the opprobrium attached to the term "outside agitator" rises, it may become impossible for anyone known as an organizer to play any public role whatsoever, which would make it necessary to blur the distinction between organizer and indigenous leader far more than was done in the MWRO. This, of course, could only be done by individuals whose skin color was the same as that of the membership. (A leading white community organizer once joked, "If I were only black, I'd be a folk hero." In all likelihood he had no more than half his tongue in his cheek when he said this.)

It has become a commonplace to associate the term "white radical" with a middle-class background. In this respect, the MWRO staff followed directly in the footsteps of the whites in CORE,[8] SNCC,[9] the SDS of the mid-1960s,[10]

and the leaders of Vietnam Summer.[11] All but one of the white MWRO staff
members described their parents as middle class, upper middle class, or lower
middle class—the one exception claimed a working class background. (Of five
black organizers, three identified their parents as middle class and one each
chose the terms lower class or poor.)

The Boston model was designed to minimize the impact of differences
in class—as well as race—between the organizer, recruiters, and potential members through the device of a two-man doorknocking team that included one
person of the same background as those being recruited. New staff members
could afford to "be themselves" since the bulk of the recruiting pitch was
delivered by a welfare recipient who described the organization in her own
words and thus overcame racial and other background differences that might
be reflected in mannerisms of speech. Those MWRO organizers who showed
discomfort "on the doors" despite the presence of these recipient recruiters
were strongly urged to consider playing some other role within the organization.

The MWRO staff was slightly older than the members of the college-based
radical organizations of the 1960s, but the bulk of the staff were either still in
college or recent college graduates, which proved beneficial to the MWRO. Since
the majority of the staff were young and without family or business responsibilities, once they were provided with a minimal level of support they could be
available virtually any time night or day for organizing work.

Neither the fact that the MWRO staff were a bit older than previous radical
and militant groups, nor the fact that they were slightly younger than most of
the members they were trying to recruit appears to have had much direct impact
on either the Boston model organizing drives or the subsequent efforts at local
group maintenance. The closeness of the MWRO organizers to campus life did
have one major indirect influence, however. More than half of all MWRO staff
members reported some organizing experience prior to joining the organization; most of these initial organizing experiences had taken place with campus
groups, many of them with the Students for a Democratic Society.

Given the fact that the MWRO membership consisted almost exclusively
of women, the sex of the organizers must have had some importance. The few
black female MWRO organizers found it relatively easy to move beyond the
normal organizer role into a more active leadership position. Those lay leaders
who set down qualifications for their organizers invariably requested women,
perhaps to avoid having to take orders from males. In the case of male organizers, there was the possibility of a romantic or other liaison between a staff
person and a member. Veterans of civil rights and other movement organizations have at times spoken of the complications introduced whenever organizers and members became involved in such liaisons. Pastreich was aware of
this difficulty and was forceful in facing up to it. Among the few inflexible
instructions given to new recruits to the staff was the following dictum.

No sleeping with the ladies. If I ever find out that anyone has been doing something like that, I'll do everything in my power to get you out of this organization so fast you won't ever know what happened to you.

Although it is understandably difficult to gain reliable information about adherence to this rule, there is no available evidence that the MWRO even had any difficulties in this area.

The fact that the MWRO staff was evenly divided between men and women added to the sense of community that developed among the organizers. In addition to the many close friendships that were formed while working for the MWRO (and that have continued long after those involved left the organization), there were two marriages between members of the staff.

The Motives of the MWRO Staff

Although the immediate reasons for joining the MWRO staff were largely idiosyncratic, most members' explanations for deciding to participate were related to the organization's proven record of effectiveness. Nearly 60 per cent referred to a desire to learn how to organize or to the MWRO reputation as the most successful grassroots organization they knew about. Those seeking to learn how to organize presumably chose the MWRO because it was so successful and thus both of these reasons boil down to a single conclusion: the ability of the MWRO to attract staff was largely dependent upon its ability to demonstrate that it could "produce." This is of course precisely the same reasons why most members decided to participate.

What was perhaps most striking about the explanations given by MWRO staff members for decisions to participate was the absence of references to the presumed ends of the welfare rights movement—that is, to improvement in the lives of welfare recipients. As is shown in Table 5-1, only 7 of 45 respondents explained their decision in terms of changing the welfare system or bringing benefits to welfare recipients. This stands in sharp contrast with the 22 respondents who made direct reference to the *process* of community organization. It was almost as if the means were justifying the ends: formal goals were less important than building poor people's organizations. Staff members discussed the nuances of organizing drives endlessly, they rarely mentioned such programs as a guaranteed annual income or President Nixon's Family Assistance Plan.

It is likely that many of those who gave other responses were also attracted to the MWRO because of its demonstrated effectiveness. To the extent that this is true, the pressure on the MWRO to prove itself would even be greater than we have already suggested.

Table 5-1

"Why Did You Decide to Work for the MWRO?" [a]

Respondents making direct mention of organizing	22[b]
(Joined to learn how to organize or because support goal of organizing the poor)	
Respondents making reference to the effectiveness of the MWRO	8
(Often with indirect references to organizing)	
Respondents making reference to changing the welfare system or improving the life of poor people	7[b]
Respondents indicating a previous commitment to the welfare rights movement elsewhere in the country	3
Miscellaneous responses	7
TOTAL RESPONDENTS	45[b]

[a]Typical examples of responses and categories assigned include:

Direct mention of organizing: "I heard that Bill Pastreich was one of the best organizers in the country and my interest was learning organizing." "The idea of organized poor folks turns me on."

Other responses making reference to effectiveness: "It's where it's at." "It's involved in grassroots action without excessive rhetoric."

Changing the welfare system: "To make a permanent contribution to the underprivileged." "It's a good cause." "Because women get a dirty deal on welfare."

[b]Of 45 respondents, 2 gave answers that were classified as both directly mentioning organizing and making reference to changing the system: "Client organization is the only way to change the system," and "[Because I favor] material gains for people and organizing for social change."

The importance of the positive feedback that the MWRO organizers received from their efforts cannot be given enough stress. Many organizers such as the leaders of the Berkeley Vietnam Day Committee in 1965 have viewed community organization as an essentially thankless task, appropriate only for those with a good deal of patience:

> At least a march is concrete, they rationalize, while community organizing or building a grass-roots political movement offers little theory and little concrete satisfaction, either to students or dropouts who have only recently began to think in political or even social terms.[12]

For people with these concerns, a Boston model organizing drive with its built-in guarantee of a large turnout at the first meeting and the virtual guarantee of a successful first confrontation held an unrivaled attractiveness. The repetition of "benefit-of-the-month club" drives with fewer and fewer members turning out did not prove to be particularly satisfying however. As was indicated in Chapter 4, these attitudes on the part of the MWRO organizers were a contributing factor to the rapid growth and slow decline that was typical of most MWRO affiliates.

For some MWRO organizers, the effectiveness of the organization was important only indirectly; what concerned them most was being a part of an energetic organization that seemed to be doing things and attracting publicity. Jacobs and Landau have given several examples of this phenomenon in other contexts:

> The majority of SDS members, then and today [i.e., 1966] are anti-ideological, and are in SDS because that's where the action is. . . . The Free Speech Movement at Berkeley . . . attracted older radicals who saw it as providing an opportunity to be where the action was.[13]

American youth no longer speak of "where the action is," but this is precisely the same motivation expressed by the MWRO organizer who said he decided to work for the MWRO because "it's where it's at."

MWRO staff members almost never discussed their motives and long-range goals with each other. Pastreich thought this was deliberate and that "if everybody knew why everyone else were here, a lot of people might quit." It is more likely that ideology and long-range goals were not discussed simply because few people were concerned with such matters; their attention was on the short-run. All that was asked of MWRO staff members was that they show loyalty to the organization, reliability in carrying out orders, common sense, and a potential for relating to the welfare recipient membership. In short, all that was ever asked of them is that they demonstrate competance in the tasks of organizing.

At the same time, however, it should be noted that Pastreich's attitude towards recruiting was not like that attributed to Charles Sherrod of SNCC: "I don't care who the heck he is—if he's willing to come down on the front lines and bring his body along with me to die—then he's welcome."[14] Pastreich would not have accepted anyone he knew to be a Communist (or a member of the Progressive Labor Party) for his staff, not because he opposed them ideologically but simply because of the discredit they might bring to his organizing effort if others found out about them. As it was, no one known to be Communists or members of the PLP ever applied to join the MWRO staff.

Word about the MWRO spread throughout the Boston area and to a lesser extent across the country largely by personal contacts as well as the mass media. But the factors that led those who had heard about the organization to join were

not goal related. They were attracted by their relatively unambiguous performance measures that showed MWRO organizers could "deliver"—they could
build groups and win victories.

Once an organizer had spent a few weeks or so on the staff, other inducements began to grow increasingly important. These included a heightened sense
of the importance of the job of organizing welfare recipients, the continuing
opportunities for personal development and advancement, and the satisfactions
from warm relationships with fellow staff members. Most of these were offered
in the past by other movement organizations, but Pastreich and his successors
were well-attuned to their potency and made conscious efforts to develop them.

Pastreich took every available opportunity to impress his staff with the
overriding priority attached to the work being carried out by the MWRO. He
once told this writer (in confidence) that

> Lots of times I begin to think that the Vietnam war may be more
> important than welfare rights. But I never tell anyone on the staff. I
> try to convince each of them that what they are doing is the most
> important thing in the world right now.

The relative isolation of the majority of the MWRO staff from the community
at large and from activities other than welfare rights made it easier to maintain
this stress on the overarching importance of welfare rights. When Pastreich
would tell those present at a staff meeting that "there are few grassroots organizers in the entire country better than those sitting in this room tonight," few
in his audience had independent sources of information to evaluate his remarks.
In short, Pastreich possessed a single-minded devotion to the task of building an
effective grassroots organization that caused him to weigh carefully the impact of
every word he uttered to friend or foe, to the head of a welfare department, or to
his own organizers.

The overarching importance of the work organizing welfare mothers was not
only stressed by Pastreich but also exemplified by his personal behavior and that
of his immediate successor. He never left any doubt that for him, welfare rights
came first and everything else—including his own wife and children—came second. The self-sacrifice of the MWRO staff director made it easier for him to
make demands of others without risking personal criticism.

Tension between movement responsibilities and family life has been observed
in many organizations. Keniston wrote that

> "the married radical is often faced with the difficult decision whether
> to place his wife or his radical work first. . . . Marriage family life and
> an established occupation do not mix well with active Movement
> work."[15]

Bell reports that a major cause of high turnover in CORE chapters was "the need to appease family complaints about the member's continual absence from the home."[16]

The MWRO also offered its staff members a vehicle for self-development in a context free of most adult responsibilities. This is the same motive discussed by Kenneth Keniston in his study of the Vietnam Summer organization:

> Most were still deliberately attempting to change themselves as
> people, to educate themselves as radicals, and to train themselves
> for greater political effectiveness.[17]

Jacobs and Landau have made a similar observation for "the Movement" as a whole.[18] This conception of the MWRO staff as a way station on the path between college student and traditional adult career and family responsibilities appears to support Keniston's theorizing about "youth" as an "emergent stage of life," but any final judgment about the applicability of the concept must be paid off until enough time has passed to see whether MWRO staff members had engaged in organizing for only a year or two, as the functional equivalent of a Peace Corps assignment, or whether they became career community organizers.

Just under one-third of the MWRO staff specifically indicated that they had chosen to work for the MWRO for reasons of personal development and education; they came to learn how to organize. Most of the internal activities of the MWRO staff, especially the twice weekly staff meetings, responded to these needs to an extent far exceeding that which would have been necessary merely to carry out the everyday activities of the organization. In addition to regular discussions of the Boston model, the assumptions behind its nuances, and possible modifications of it, time at staff meetings was devoted to discussion of other strategies of community organizing. MWRO organizers were encouraged to consider alternative models and were promised organizational resources to try to implement them. (As already indicated, however, none of these alternative models ever got off the ground.)

The MWRO staff thus functioned as a "school for community organizers" by providing its members with regular opportunities to meet informally in seminar-like sessions with leading community organizers both from within the welfare rights movement and from other groups as well. Key figures on the national staff of the welfare rights movement such as George Wiley and Hulbert James led such sessions nearly every time they were in Boston. Pastreich himself made repeated trips to Boston, after he had resigned from the MWRO, in order to lead "training sessions."

Members of the MWRO staff also helped plan training sessions for Boston area VISTA volunteers and saw to it that all MWRO organizers were invited. The leaders of these training sessions—including such men as Saul Alinsky and Warren Haggstrom—often supplemented the general sessions with meetings open to MWRO staff only. Whenever leading practitioners and theoreticians of community organizing such as Richard Cloward and Frances Fox Piven were known to be in Boston, they were invited to attend MWRO staff meetings. More often than not, they accepted the invitations.

The lively exchanges at these sessions provided intellectual stimulation to the staff as well as an antidote against becoming overly concerned with the particularistic problems of organizing welfare recipients in Massachusetts in the late 1960s. This combination of exposure to leading community organizers, distribution of mimeographed copies of their writings, intensive "field work" experience in the building of a movement, the personal and group supervision of Pastreich, as well as the twice weekly staff meetings provided the equivalent of a course in community organizing unmatched by any formal educational institution in the country. Regional meetings and national conventions of the welfare rights movement provided an opportunity for both professional and social interaction with colleagues from other parts of the country along the lines of the conventions offered by other academic and professional groups. In sum, the MWRO provided much of what a formal graduate education should offer, but in a less structured atmosphere. It did not, however, provide a broad enough perspective on the welfare rights goals and values to enable it to overcome its basic problems in organizational maintenance.

The affiliation of the MWRO with a larger welfare rights movement gave its staff members opportunities for advancement that would not have otherwise been available. It was relatively common for organizers to move from second level positions in Massachusetts to positions of more responsibility elsewhere. "Alumni" of the MWRO staff have served as chief organizers for the welfare rights movement in the states of Indiana, Rhode Island, Vermont, Washington, and Arkansas. Members of the MWRO staff were offered key positions on the National Welfare Rights Organization staff in Washington, D.C., that enabled them to work on the national level if they so chose. Although it is relatively easy for talented organizers to move from one movement to another once they have made a name for themselves, the presence of a national structure in the welfare rights movement contributed to the rise to positions of influence of those members of the MWRO staff who had not yet developed any reputations.

The MWRO affiliation with a broader movement and attendant opportunity for geographic mobility may also have been a factor in helping its staff face the disappointment of its inability to translate grassroots organization into political power. When there were setbacks in Massachusetts, the staff could still derive satisfaction from legal victories in Washington, D.C., and a combination of direct action and court activities in the state of Nevada.

The close personal ties that developed among MWRO staff members provided another reason for individuals to stay with the organization. Feelings of friendship and camaraderie appear to have played a vital role in many previous civil rights and New Left activist organizations in the past. The SDS was once described as "more than an organization; it is a community of friends."[19] Keniston has linked this friendship motive with the isolation of movement groups from the wide community:

> One consequence of the inward focus of movement groups— whether in Mississippi, the slums of Northern cities, or the National Headquarters of Vietnam Summer—is the intensification of the relationships between their members and the development of *strong feelings of solidarity*, closeness, intimacy, and openness within the group. . . . Especially when working in hostile communities or when doing extremely frustrating work like community organizing in the inner city, members of the same group developed a mutual affection, akin to that of soldiers who have survived the same battle.[20]

The tendency towards isolation increased as individuals played more important roles within the MWRO that threatened to consume every waking moment of their time. Pastreich's isolation from the community at large was the greatest of all. Despite his acknowledgement of the importance of mass media to protest activities, he had no idea of the call letters of Boston's leading radio and television stations. His lack of outside contacts was illustrated during a fund-raising effort involving the raffling off of a color television set. As sales lagged, Pastreich urged the MWRO staff to spend as much time as possible peddling raffle tickets to their friends and acquaintances. Half jokingly he volunteered that he could be of no help in this endeavor because "the only people I know in this town are welfare recipients and you organizers."

But whatever their ties to others, the MWRO staff spent a good deal of time together even when "not on the job." For a long period of time, a weekend (co-ed) touch football game was as much a part of the schedule for the group as the staff meetings. Successful demonstrations were often capped by parties attended primarily by MWRO staff members.

Somewhat surprisingly, most MWRO organizers remained unaware of the importance of this motivation. At one time, dissension in the organization forced the closing of the MWRO storefront headquarters in Cambridge. Despite the fact that virtually all the normal activities of the organization could have continued using private homes for temporary meeting places, there was strong sentiment among most staff members to take whatever risks were involved in re-opening the storefront as soon as possible. Only the most perceptive organizers saw that the drive to do this was based on the desire to have a place for the pleasures of informal interaction during the working day.

The feelings of solidarity were relatively less important for the MWRO than they probably were for many other movement groups because they did not have to bear the burden of motivating continued participation by themselves. But when the pleasures of associating with close friends were superimposed upon the

motives relating to proven effectiveness and enrollment in a "school for organizers," the combination was a powerful one.

Personal ties between local group organizers and the lay leaders of their
groups also served to induce continued participation. Many organizers felt personally responsible for the local groups they had founded and the lay leaders
who came to depend upon their assistance. These motives were not generally
strong enough to convince a staff member to stay on indefinitely when all other
attempts at persuasion failed. But they were usually sufficient to convince
organizers to postpone their departures until "the next major demonstration"
if not until the new group was "on its own feet." While denying that such senti-
ments should motivate a truly professional community organizer, Pastreich and
his successors did not hesitate to try to utilize them to keep the staff together as
long as was possible. This motivation also appears to have been common to
other movement groups as well. Jacobs and Landau cite the identical sentiment
in a veteran SNCC member: "I would leave Mississippi now and forever, except
that I owe something to the people I got involved."[21]

The Values of the MWRO Staff

Since the MWRO staff shared much of the background and motivations as
earlier civil rights and New Left activists, one might expect that they would have
also shared their beliefs and attitudes as well. While this was true in some areas,
there were sharp differences between the priorities expressed by the MWRO
organizers and those of activists in such groups as SNCC, CORE, SDS, and Vietnam Summer. In part, these differences resulted from the formal goals of the
different movement groups and the resulting difference in incentives offered.
But the most crucial determinant of MWRO values—and the fact that differentiated the welfare rights movement from most other organizations in its field—
was the presence of relatively unambiguous performance measures for the group's
efforts: dues-paying memberships, turnout of regular meetings, and disbursement of thousands of dollars worth of supplementary welfare payments to its
members.

Community organization—like many endeavors outside of the profit-making
sector of the economy—is a field that normally lacks even a semblance of an
unambiguous performance measure. The inability of would-be organizers to
mobilize more than a handful of people had often reduced them to giving assess-
ments of their performance in terms of "numbers of lives touched." The strong
positive feedback that MWRO staff members received from the Boston model
organizing drives stood in sharp contrast to this situation. The presence of these
measures intensified pressures to "produce" in a manner that would relate to
them, and thus tended to divert or distort competing organizational values. As
a result, the MWRO priorities were displaced away from the creation of stable

pressure groups towards successive replication and perfection of the techniques involved in maximizing turnout at the first meetings and first confrontations during organizing drives.[a] The obvious success of the Boston model drives thus contributed to the failure of these groups to survive because the drives virtually monopolized the time and attention of the MWRO staff to the detriment of modifying the model to develop other techniques to maintain groups.

As was suggested in Chapter 2, this displacement within the MWRO directly paralleled the NWRO Poverty Rights Action Center's concentration upon organizing welfare recipients and thus abandoning the broader goal of organizing all poor people. Welfare recipients were organized in large part simply because this was so much easier to accomplish—and to demonstrate its accomplishment.

The availability of these performance measures and the resulting pressures to have a high rating on them served to intensify MWRO adherence to many of the values commonly associated with the activists of the 1960s. The pressure to produce required a willingness to set aside preconceived notions and rigid long-range strategies. The MWRO staff thus followed in the footsteps of earlier activists who rejected any detailed blueprints of what they hoped the future would look like and how precisely to attain that hoped for future. Howard Zinn's description of SNCC workers in the early years of the decade are just as applicable to the MWRO staff at its close:

> They have no party, no ideology, no creed. They have no clear idea of a blueprint for a future society. . . . [They] have not become followers of any dogma and have not pledged themselves to any rigid ideological system.[22]

Kenneth Keniston similarly reports that among the leaders of Vietnam Summer, the term ideology was almost always used pejoratively, an attitude he takes to be a defining characteristic of the New Left.[23]

The MWRO staff followed directly in this tradition, and put down attempts at ideological justification for a course of action as "radical bullshit." Conversation at staff meetings and informal discussions were notably devoid of reference to long-range consequence; only the tactics were important.

MWRO staff members agreed that it was important to build a network of strong local welfare rights organizations, but few organizers had any idea what might be accomplished with this network once it was in place. This uncertainty was reflected in the deep divisions within the MWRO staff over whether all their scarce resources should be concentrated upon direct organization of welfare

---

[a]The criterion of numbers was not a perfectly unambiguous performance measure for community organizers because it was never clear what obstacles the organizer had to overcome in getting the turnout. For this reason, previously made reputations tended to maintain themselves. But while not perfect, the criterion of numbers was far superior to those measures employed by other groups.

recipients or whether strong efforts should be made to build alliances with other groups. This second alternative, usually referred to as "middle-class work" by the staff was generally downgraded. As might be expected, attitudes towards building alliances were related to the roles played within the organization and in particular with the amount of contact each role afforded with non-recipients. The local group organizers showed far less concern with building alliances than did the inner circle. The central staff members assigned to "middle-class work" gave this goal an even higher rating.

This flexibility with respect to long-range goals and short-run tactics was mirrored by the general openness towards the future that MWRO staff members shared with many of their predecessors in other movement organizations. Half the MWRO organizers interviewed in the winter of 1969–70 did not know if they would be on the staff at the beginning of the next school year. More than half of those who began work in the summer of 1970 had no idea whether they would remain in the fall. Keniston saw this same uncertainty in the leaders of Vietnam Summer:

> In late August 1967, fewer than half of those interviewed . . . knew for sure what they would be doing on September 15. Those that did know were planning to resume their educations and had no plans beyond the completion of their studies.[24]

Despite the fact that the majority of the MWRO staff members were college graduates, few of them were certain about their ultimate career goals. Roughly half of the staff responded negatively when asked, "Do you have a career goal in mind?" One quarter chose community organization and the remainder were divided among teaching, law, and the other professions. This indecision about future plans gives further corroboration to our speculations as to the relevance of Keniston's concept of the "stage of youth" to the MWRO staff.

Despite these similarities between the attitudes and values of the MWRO staff and those of previous movement groups, the availability of the unambiguous performance measure in the welfare rights movement (and its absence in these other cases) led to a number of important divergences. The most obvious of these was the openness of the MWRO organizers with the problems of gaining power and their willingness to modify absolute moral standards in favor of taking the steps necessary to succeed in gaining power, that is to maximize the attendance at welfare rights meetings and demonstrations.

Jack Newfield made the following observations about the SDS and the radicals of the 1960s:

> When SDSers are posed with a possible strategy, they ask themselves not "Is it workable?" . . . They ask themselves "Is it right to do this?"

> The new radicals . . . are not particularly concerned with power or success, but rather with absolute moral consequences like love, justice, equality, and freedom.[25]

The MWRO staff, on the other hand, was not only unafraid to talk about power but was also close to unanimous in giving the goal "building the power of the poor" their highest priority. The ranking of MWRO goals is given in Table 5-2. The associated goal of "politicizing the mothers" received the second highest rating.

Earlier movement organizations may have turned away from concern with power because it appeared unattainable. The SDS Port Huron statement speaks of bringing people "out of isolation and into community" and helping them in "finding meaning in personal life." The Vietnam Summer organization was seeking to mobilize American public opinion against the war in Southeast Asia and eventually to politicize vast new constituencies to a radical view of society. None of these goals was very attainable in the short run, and hence it is possible that these groups therefore turned towards concern with inherent rightness of purpose in order to cover up these weaknesses. The MWRO got results and thus had less need to philosophize about purity of motives and correctness of procedures.

Table 5-2
MWRO Staff Ratings Given to Organizational Goals

	Rating[a]	Priority[b]
A. Getting goods for the mothers	2.6	11
B. "Politicizing" the mothers	4.5	2
C. Building strong local groups	4.2	3
D. Building a strong statewide organization	4.1	4
E. Building a strong national organization	4.1	5
F. Building the power of the poor	4.7	1
G. Building middle-class support	2.9	10
H. Laying the groundwork for "the revolution"	3.3	8
I. Gaining adequate income (for the poor)	3.9	6
J. Training individuals in organizing	3.6	7
K. Leadership training to eventually eliminate the need for (non-recipient) organizers	3.1	9

[a]Figures represent the mean numerical response of the staff when asked to rate the importance of a given goal from 1 (low) to 5 (high).

[b]Priorities represent a numerical ordering of the ratings.

Many MWRO organizers questioned Saul Alinsky's article of faith that "if people have the power, the opportunity to act, in the long run they will, most of the time, reach the right decisions."[26] But this did not negate their belief that the problems of the poor could not be solved *without* a transfer to them of political influence. In the short run, MWRO organizers felt, the only way to effect this transfer of power was to build poor people's organizations. This point reinforces the earlier observation that the MWRO staff was more concerned with the process of organizing than with any formal goals that organization might accomplish. As is shown in Table 5-2, the achievement of adequate income for all, the formal goal of the National Welfare Rights Organization stood only sixth in the ranking of organizational priorities, below the process-oriented ends of building power and politicizing the general membership and below the agreed upon means by which this could be accomplished—the building of the organization on the local, state, and national levels.

The MWRO staff's understanding of the nature of power and its importance in bringing about social change were based on the thought of Saul Alinsky and Warren Haggstrom. Both of these men had a great impact upon Bill Pastreich, and it was through Pastreich that these men exerted their influence. Alinsky taught that the questions of power had to be addressed if people wanted to improve their conditions:

> A fundamental difference between liberals and radicals is to be found in the issue of power. Liberals fear power and its application. They . . . fail to realize that only through the achievement and constructive use of power can people better themselves.[27]

The theoretical basis for the Boston model—to the extent that there was one—can be traced to Pastreich's espousal of Haggstrom's thinking about the causes and cure for poverty. Haggstrom's writings were a prime source of the mimeographed articles about organizing that Pastreich periodically distributed to the staff. One of these contained the essence of Haggstrom's approach and hence of the Boston model itself:

> If the problem were only one of lack of money, it could be solved through provision of more and better paying jobs for the poor, increased minimum wage levels, higher levels of welfare payments and so on. There would be, in that case, no real need for the poor to undertake any political action on their own behalf.
>
> However, since it is more likely that the problem is one of powerlessness, joint initiative by the poor on their own behalf should preceed and accompany responses from the rest of society. In practice, this initiative is likely to be most effectively exercised by powerful conflict organizations based in neighborhoods of poverty.[28]

The theoretical portion of the MWRO recruiting pitch was evidently derived
from the following passage from Saul Alinsky:

> You can get jobs, you can break segregated housing patterns.
> But you have to have power to do it, and you'll get it only through
> organization. Because power just goes to two poles—those who have
> money and those who've got people. You [poor people] haven't got
> money so your own fellow men are your only source of strength.[29]

The members of the welfare rights organizations generally ignored those sections
of the pitch that referred to power and focused almost entirely on the instructions how to get special needs grants. But for the MWRO staff, these passages
were as close to an ideology as they ever got.

The conflict between ideals and pressure to produce was nowhere greater
than in the areas of "participatory democracy," "non-leadership," and fear of
manipulation that Jack Newfield has called the definitive characteristics of the
New Left.[30] Many activist organizations have stressed their allegiance to these
ideals. In the case of the SDS in its early years, Jacobs and Landau wrote:

> It is difficult to single out those who hold authority. Leaders,
> elected and de factor, hem and haw when they are called leaders,
> for traditional authority and arbitrary decision-making are incom-
> patible with the values of the SDS staff.[31]

The Port Huron statement of the SDS is perhaps one of the most eloquent dis-
avowals of manipulation among movement groups:

> We regard men as infinitely precious and possessed of unfulfilled
> capacities for reason, freedom, and love. In affirming these principles
> we are aware of countering perhaps the dominant conceptions of man
> in the twentieth century: that he is a thing to be manipulated, and he
> is inherently incapable of directing his own affairs.[32]

Similarly the leaders of Vietnam Summer were reported to have "frowned upon"
tactics involving playing to the media despite sometimes acknowledging their
value:

> Implicit in this critique of flashiness is the assumption that it
> involved a manipulation of the people who are being organized.
> Flashiness, then, amounts to a form of exploitation.[33]

Studies of these organizations have noted the tensions created by these
ideals and the penalties paid by those attempting to reject manipulative activities while trying to maintain an action-oriented organization. Newfield has

described participatory democracy as "an effective and therapeutic organizing technique, but it is not the cornerstone for a theory of social change."[34] Keniston has noted how the desire to be unmanipulative, participatory, and equal in Vietnam Summer led to a situation in which decisions tended "to take a long time to arrive at, to become fuzzy or blurred, or not to be made at all."[35]

Pressure to produce is present in all movement organizations and all are forced to make some compromises with their ideals. These compromises appear to have been most evident in those areas where performance was most readily measurable. SNCC leaders were reported to have abandoned the value of honesty when public disclosure of a rift with Dr. Martin Luther King would have greatly hindered their fund-raising.[36] Both SNCC[37] and the Vietnam Summer leadership[38] were reported to have given up the ideal of participatory democracy in order to meet the pressing needs for some decisions to be made quickly. With success so much easier to gauge in the MWRO, the pressures to produce were inevitably greater, and thus the incentives to modify principles that might hamper organizational effectiveness were much more open and frequent. The immediate feedback from successful demonstrations and growing membership rolls had the effect of quieting misgivings among MWRO staff members.

While never denying the basic validity of openness and straightforwardness, the MWRO staff learned to come to terms with its compunctions about centralized decision-making and behind the scenes activity. They learned to accept what they saw as an unpleasant reality that selective reporting or withholding of information and a monopoly of decision-making by an inner circle were sometimes requisites of building effective poor people's organizations. They were never happy with the use of deception and remained unwilling to see themselves as "using" the poor to further personal needs and ambitions as previous exploiters of the ghetto had done. When one organizer accused another of believing that "manipulation is where it's at," everyone present laughed. But they laughed not so much because of the distastefulness of this position as because of the feeling of uneasiness that it gave them.

The MWRO staff preferred to look upon themselves as professionals, ready to do whatever was necessary to get the job done. But they could not abandon their sensitivity altogether; they maintained their ideals as much as was possible and put them aside only with great regret. While they would have preferred participatory democracy for the staff, they did accept an inner circle and one-man decision-making process. Newcomers were quickly informed that staff meetings were not to be confused with town meetings at which votes would be taken. The ideal of nonleadership was maintained, however, in a modified form: experienced staff members could expect to be consulted and their opinions would be taken seriously; and the reasoning behind a particular decision would be explained in depth in future staff meetings.

Bill Pastreich was viewed by other staff members as the prime example of this attitude. His position can be illustrated by a discussion at a staff meeting concerning an upcoming election for the MWRO lay leadership. He prefaced his remarks by asking whether anyone had any qualms about the staff involving itself in the "politicking." He then clarified his own position:

> I am asking this question not in order to take a vote on the issue.
> I am asking only to find out who shouldn't be around when the rest
> of us are making our plans.

When Pastreich left the MWRO, the staff chose a new staff director who was expected to continue Pastreich's format. When the second staff director resigned, the MWRO organizers accepted an interim leadership structure of shared responsibility only until a single individual could be recruited to take full responsibility.

The third staff director, despite strong personal doubts about the Pastreich leadership style, soon found himself reserving decision-making power (and final responsibility) for himself because, in his own words:

> *We have some important actions coming up and there are a lot of*
> *new people in the organization. There isn't enough time to teach a*
> *lot of people all the important details about putting a demonstration*
> *together. You can learn them only by taking part and following some-*
> *one else's orders. For the time being, I am therefore continuing to*
> *exercise final responsibility. All decisions will be mine.*

He would have preferred non-leadership but recognized that in paramilitary areas, such as planning and leading demonstrations, a clear chain of command is vital.

This conflict between participatory democracy and directive behavior becomes especially relevant in the determination of the goals of poor people's organizations. Many community organizers have stressed the need to take the time to learn what the people want and then help them organize to get it. Thus for example, the SDS community organization projects (the so-called ERAP program) were based on these principles:

> ERAP community organizers make no attempt to impose their
> ideas upon the poor, but rather to learn from the poor and to nurture
> indigenous leadership.[39]

Similarly, in the words of one SNCC worker,

> We're not concerned with time. We're just going to let people
> in the community know we are here, become involved in their daily
> lives, and find out what they want us to do.[40]

Although this was also close to the opinion taken by their predecessors in the Mothers for Adequate Welfare, the MWRO staff did not follow suit. The use of an organizing model based on supplementary welfare checks for furniture and clothing denied the prerequisite of learning what people wanted. Although admitting that there were local irritants that vary from location to location, Pastreich expressed the MWRO consensus with his observation that

> *People everywhere want the same things. They want food, cloth-ing, and shelter. You don't have to spend a lot of time asking them.*

The issue of whether the dependence of members of a poor people's organization upon their organizers ought to be actively discouraged is also closely related to the dilemmas of participatory democracy versus direction. Although this issue caused more ambivalence within the MWRO staff than any other one relating to ideals versus pragmatism, the staff consensus was to make sacrifices to insure tangible results. The rationale in this case was precisely the one that justified organizer domination of the Boston model first meeting:

> *The only way to end the dependence of the poor upon others is for them to develop powerful self-help organizations. But until these groups are on their feet, they remain quite fragile and the active intervention of organizers is needed.*

This is not the way many civil rights workers claim to have settled the issue. SNCC workers reportedly decided not to accompany the Amite Country Negroes, whom they had organized, to the county seat to register to vote "in order to thwart dependence upon whites."[41] Another civil rights veteran had the following recollection about his decision for not agreeing to organize a given area because he opposed the possibility of black becoming dependent upon whites:

> No matter how good an organizer I might or I might not be, there's still that same old reaction: "Now here's this powerful civil rights worker, and he can do it for us." I won't go. Send someone else.[42]

The typical MWRO organizer would have agreed with the principle of avoiding the creation of new dependency relations. But at the same time he would have feared that his absence would jeopardize the success of the demonstration or campaign. Such a failure might set his organization back irrevocably. The criterion of ensuring success required that he do the organizing work himself rather than entrust it to an indigenous worker who was less familiar with the tricks of the organizing trade.

The responses of the MWRO staff when asked to evaluate the priority of the goal "Leadership training to eventually eliminate the need for (non-recipient) organizers" reveal the ambivalence on this topic. The variance in the responses was greater than for any of the other goals that appeared in Table 5-2. Roughly one-third of the MWRO organizers gave it their lowest priority and often added that it was impossible. Slightly less than a third gave the opposite response by awarding this goal their highest rating.

The pressure to produce also led the MWRO staff's rejection of another New Left ideal, spontaneity. Newfield concludes his study of the "new radicals" with an observation that because of the radical mood grassroots insurgencies will become increasingly popular in the future. "National organizations are not the style of anarchists and improvisors."[43] The MWRO staff agreed with New-field that if one were to build organizations, romanticism and spontaneity must be curbed. But since the MWRO staff was devoted to the mass production of local welfare rights organizations, they kept improvisation within clearly defined limits.

Although conflict between MWRO staff members and lay leaders was prob-ably inevitable in view of their different motives, the organizers' adherence to the values described in this chapter undoubtedly contributed to the bitterness of the internal battles within the organization. Perhaps the staff might never have been able to convince the lay leaders of the rightness of their own attitudes towards community organization or their own set of priorities. However, had they accomplished this, the organization might have avoided its decline.

6 MWRO Lay Leadership

The crucial determinant of the role played by the MWRO lay leaders was that they were all welfare recipients. Although the bylaws of the MWRO did not specify any particular welfare program, all MWRO local group chairman (except the leader of an exclusively male wage supplement organization) and all elected members of the MWRO Executive Board were beneficiaries of the Aid to Families with Dependent Children (AFDC) program. This pattern was typical of the welfare rights movement throughout the country. Thus the lay leaders of welfare rights groups were mostly women who had young children and were dependent upon the government for their standard of living.

Being poor, most MWRO lay leaders lived in public housing or dilapidated private housing, and many lacked adequate furniture and household supplies—or at least they did before joining the organization. Regardless of their degree of political sophistication, the MWRO lay leadership, as well as the general membership, therefore tended to be most responsive towards strategies that resulted in the acquisition of material benefits.

The responsiveness towards consumer goods by both the MWRO lay leaders and general membership stood in sharp contrast to the attitudes of the MWRO staff. In joining the MWRO staff, they had chosen to give up the relative abundance of middle-class life to fulfill their idealistic goals of helping to redistribute power in American society. Ironically, fulfilling this goal within the MWRO meant helping others gain the ends they had rejected for themselves.

Because the lay leaders were poor, most did not own automobiles and, for the most part, were dependent upon staff members for transportation. The staff often used the time spent driving leaders to meetings to persuade them to take certain courses of action at those meetings. Thus even such an apparently neutral function as providing rides to meetings affected the balance of power between organizers and lay leaders. Regard for the potential influence of possessing a means of transportation can be illustrated by the case of the first meeting of a rural affiliate of the MWRO. Until corrected by the organizer, most members seemed to assure that access to an automobile should be a major prerequisite to running for office.

The MWRO leaders were female heads of households and had young children. The inability of poor women to pay for full-time babysitting services both limited the role that they could play in the organization and led to conflict with the organizers. MWRO lay leaders continually used the excuse of family responsibilities whenever organizers pressed them to take a more active

role in the day-to-day work of the movement. Their requests for allocation of
organizational funds to pay for babysitters were refused by the staff on the
grounds that the payments would have consumed a considerable proportion of
the total organizational budget.

Therefore the MWRO leaders often brought their children along to meetings and demonstrations. While the presence of young children often added to
the effectiveness of demonstrations by adding to the bedlam, the children did
disrupt the internal planning meetings of the organization. On many occasions,
MWRO staff members were diverted from more important tasks to amuse the
children of lay leaders so that some organizational business might be carried out.

Although the MWRO lay leaders were all welfare recipients, they were not
typical welfare recipients. They differed from the average Massachusetts AFDC
recipient—and in all likelihood from the general membership as well—in a number of ways—that is, there was a lessened frequency of many of the traits commonly associated with "lower-class culture" or the "culture of poverty."

To begin with, the MWRO lay leadership were considerably better educated
than the average AFDC recipient in the state. Roughly three-fourths were high
school graduates. By contrast, only 1 in 4 Massachusetts AFDC recipients had
completed 12 years of schooling.[1] In fact, the median number of years of school
completed for all Americans over 25 years of age in 1969 was only 12.1.[2]

Numerous studies have reported a negative correlation between social class
and voluntary association membership.[3] MWRO leaders however tended to be
active not only in welfare rights but in other groups as well. Eleven of 16 leaders
interviewed had *already* been members of other organizations before they joined
their local welfare rights affiliate, and a number of these had been officers of the
organizations. Three others became active in other groups after their experiences
with the MWRO; the welfare rights was the only major organizational activity
for only two of those interviewed. In addition, the MWRO lay leaders appear to
have participated in the wider political process more actively than expected. All
but one of those interviewed indicated that they were registered voters.

The MWRO leadership differed from those generally thought to have a culture of poverty both in their backgrounds and plans for the future. Lower-class
culture is generally considered to be handed down from generation to generation, but the majority of the leaders indicated that their fathers held steady
working-class jobs, and a significant number came from white-collar and professional backgrounds. Three leaders were daughters of a certified public accoun-
tant, an employee of a public relations firm, and a doctor, respectively. The
leaders themselves had all at one time or another worked full-time, and if it had
not been for their children, most leaders would have returned to their jobs in
offices and factories.

Edward Banfield has suggested that attitude towards the future should be
taken as a defining characteristic of class culture. For him, the lower classes are
those who show an inability to discipline themselves to sacrifice present for

future satisfaction.[4] Although some leaders showed tendencies in this direction, they were not normally future oriented. When leaders were asked what
they would do if the Welfare Department paid them a bonus of $5000, nearly
half responded in terms of setting aside the money for their children's education or using it as a down payment on a home. Intentions are not the equivalent of actions, but these indications of concern for the future are at least
suggestive.

For all of these reasons, it seems that the MWRO leadership was drawn
disproportionately from among middle- and working-class women who had
some personal misfortune that resulted in their appearance on the welfare rolls.
Basically, they were not the "lower-class poor"; they were the "accidental
poor." For these people, organizations such as the MWRO have the potential
to help a significant proportion of welfare recipients improve themselves and
assume positions of prominence in the community. One cannot assume that
these potentialities apply to *all* welfare recipients or all of those living in
poverty.

While the MWRO statewide leadership comprised virtually all racial and
ethnic groups in the poverty population of the state, it was primarily dominated by blacks from Boston. The reasons for this can be attributed to the
underlying principles of the Boston model. Given the time-consuming nature of
doorknocking and the difficulties in arranging transportation, MWRO organizers found it easiest to build poor people's organizations in those areas in
which the potential membership was most highly concentrated. Although only
one-third of the state's welfare recipients lived in Boston, more than half of
the members who were recruited in the MWRO's first year lived in that city's
high rise public housing projects. Despite the later decline in membership, the
lay leaders from these groups, centered around the Boston housing projects,
retained their power almost throughout the history of the statewide organization. The early MWRO emphasis on Boston's largest black housing projects
contributed to the racial composition of the statewide leadership. Although
the Boston welfare recipient population was roughly divided equally between
whites and non-whites, the MWRO had only one major white leader from
Boston.

The bi-racial composition of the MWRO statewide leadership provided the
opportunity to down play or to stress the organization's black majority in
accordance with the audience. On the one hand, the MWRO drew praise from
many potential supporters and contributors by its rejection of racial rhetoric.
Whenever possible, the MWRO delegations to public hearings and church or
social welfare groups were racially mixed. But at the same time, the dominant
role of the blacks within that leadership preserved the option of stressing the
ghetto base of the movement, and hence the threat of riot. Only blacks could
effectively raise that threat and thus despite the white face or two at the forefront of the leadership phalanx, all statewide chairmen—with a single exception

lasting only a few weeks—were blacks who resided in the heart of Boston's ghettos. Despite the fact that some white lay leaders were as politically sophisticated as their black counterparts, none of them seriously considered running for the statewide chairmanship precisely for this reason.

For the most part, however, the race of the lay leaders made no difference. Although the white suburban membership of the MWRO showed a greater initial reluctance to take part in militant demonstrations than their black counterparts from Boston and Springfield, this difference was not reflected in the MWRO statewide leadership, all of whom had been in the organization for some time. The white leaders showed no less enthusiasm for militant tactics than did the blacks.

The Motives of the Lay Leaders

Two factors explained the decisions of most MWRO lay leaders to join welfare rights organizations and to continue to play active roles within them: the desire for material benefits, which was also the prime incentive for the general membership, and the personal satisfactions that come from being a leader. As was true of the MWRO staff, the lay leaders appeared only minimally concerned with such major programmatic changes in public assistance as President Nixon's proposed Family Assistance Plan.

The vast majority of MWRO members joined in order to receive supplementary welfare benefits and participated in further activities only insofar as they were related to the receipt of these benefits. Although only two leaders admitted this motivation in response when questioned on why they initially joined, the desire for furniture and household supplies undoubtedly played a major role in the initial decisions of nearly all lay leaders. On a number of occasions when they had a choice between a course of action that would maximize the certainty of their receipt of special needs grants or one that would further the long-run growth and power of the statewide organization, the majority of MWRO lay leaders opted for the former. For example, the Massachusetts Welfare Department had announced modest guidelines for school clothing shortly before the largest series of coordinated demonstrations in MWRO history was scheduled to get under way. Most MWRO lay leaders opposed welfare office confrontations for further benefits for fear that these confrontations would jeopardize the benefits already promised. At that point, the coordinated campaign had to be cancelled.

It is difficult to assess the extent to which members of the MWRO statewide and local group leadership joined the movement specifically with the idea of becoming an officer. Over two-thirds of the leadership responded to the question "why did you want to become an officer?" by saying "I didn't". Each one expressed some variation of the theme that they were chosen by the membership. In many cases, MWRO organizers came into contact with women whom they considered promising in the course of their doorknocking activities and encouraged them to first become doorknockers and then run for local group office. Organizers also exerted subtle influence in favor of these women prior to and during local group elections.

On the other hand, there were some leaders who needed no prodding to run for office. A number of the lay leaders, unlike the bulk of the general membership, had joined the organization on their own initiative rather than through direct persuasion from the staff during an organizing drive. Most MWRO members had never heard about welfare rights or thought about joining it until doorknockers had come to their doors to try to recruit them. The leadership were, however, disproportionately "self-starters." Having learned about welfare rights or the formation of a new group from friends or relatives, from members of other organizations to which they belonged, or in the newspapers and on the radio and television, they needed no persuasion to attend. They saw an opportunity and quickly moved to take advantage of it. This fact, which emphasizes the differences between the MWRO leadership and the other welfare recipients, can be illustrated by the following explanation of how one of the top leaders first became involved:

> A friend told me about Bill Pastreich and welfare rights so I cut a class at Northeastern [University] to attend the first meeting and to find out some more.

Many of these self-starters participated as doorknockers in organizing drives, and since clothes, furniture, and household supplies could be acquired simply by attending the first meeting and following confrontation, one can assume that having spent long hours knocking on their neighbors' doors, they had other motivations as well as the desire for tangible benefits. By the close of a drive, most doorknockers felt that they deserved public recognition and many assumed, without needing encouragement, that they would be elected to local group office.

While the general membership was asked only to "come and get it," much more was asked of the leader in terms of time and effort. Additional inducements were therefore needed to elicit their continuing activity. These inducements ranged from additional material benefits and services from both the Welfare Department and the MWRO staff, the excitement and satisfaction derived from engaging in personal relationships with other leaders, and those benefits that generally accrue to office-holders, such as seeing one's activities reported (and one's picture) in the mass media.

The most obvious of the additional benefits received by the MWRO lay leaders was deferential treatment at their local welfare offices. Many lay leaders received especially generous amounts of special needs grants; all received increased respect. In some cases, this resulted from the desire on the part of caseworkers to avoid alienating a woman who might return at the head of a potential mob. In others, there were attempts at cooptation. An additional increment of benefits was given to the lay leaders simply because they had become so well informed about the welfare regulations; they showed little hesitancy in appealing their cases to supervisors—or even state welfare officials—when dissatisfied with the decision of a caseworker.

The MWRO staff was aware both of the burdens of leadership for welfare recipients and of their own dependence upon these women if the organization was to function as they wished it to; they were therefore free in doing favors for the leaders. Lay leaders with individual grievances at the welfare office often got their organizers to act as advocates. MWRO statewide leaders had a high priority on the services of the lawyers on the MWRO staff, whether or not their legal problems dealt with welfare. Lay leaders could rely on staff members for transportation for all organizational activities; they always got door-to-door service.

The favors provided by the staff often went beyond the organizational context. The more important a mother perceived herself to be to the organization, the more demands—including a wide variety of personal favors—she was apt to make on MWRO staff members. It was not unusual for key leaders to ask for babysitters or rides for their children to and from school. Veteran staff members often repeated stories of how an early leader had persuaded organizers to do her shopping.

In addition to goods and services, the MWRO staff arranged for direct cash compensation for a number of lay leaders by arranging their enrollment in the Massachusetts Commonwealth Service Corps, a state-run VISTA-like program. On occasion, MWRO leaders were rewarded with the opportunity for free or low-cost travel throughout the state and elsewhere in the country as well; over 50 leaders and members of the MWRO—nearly 2 per cent of the total membership—attended the National Welfare Rights Organization Convention in Detroit in August 1969.

The MWRO lay leadership also received a variety of intangible benefits from their positions in the organization. Many leaders derived a good deal of satisfaction from the close working relationships they had developed with other members of the leadership. In some cases, local group chairmen recruited their friends and relatives to help with organizational duties and helped them to become leaders as well. In other cases, new friendships were made among the women who met regularly to carry out local group business. Discussion of business invariably became intertwined with personal matters during meetings of MWRO lay leaders, and despite bitter disputes and power struggles, a genuine affection grew among MWRO lay leadership.

Lastly, and perhaps most importantly, most MWRO officers derived a good deal of satisfaction from the mere fact of being leaders—from the prestige that

comes from sitting at the head table at meetings and from sitting behind a desk
in the local group office. They valued the opportunities to meet personally
with officials ranging from the directors of their local welfare offices and local
politicians, to state officials including the governor. They also enjoyed the
recognition that comes from speaking to the press and appearing on television—
especially the direct feedback from those who had read about them or actually
seen them on the local news.

The importance of this concern for public recognition can be illustrated
by the nature of the involvement of the MWRO statewide leadership in planning
the largest rally in the group's history, the celebration of the third anniversary
of the welfare rights movement held on the Boston Common on June 30, 1969.
Although the MWRO Executive Board members were kept appraised of, and
had to approve all plans, the only issue that held their sustained interest was the
identity of the major speakers. The MWRO organizers favored recruiting nation-
ally known figures to speak on the grounds that this would be most attractive
to the mass media. The statewide leadership strongly opposed this notion
because, in the words of one of them:

> We think that we should be the main speakers. The others are
> just a bunch of headline grabbers while we have been doing all the
> hard work.

The final plans for the rally called for a combination of outside speakers—featur-
ing Dr. Benjamin Spock—and two or three MWRO lay leaders. In fact, however,
all but one of the statewide leaders somehow found their way to the podium to
address the crowd. (The division of labor and credit between MWRO leaders and
staff dictated that no MWRO organizer spoke at the rally, although George Wiley
of the NWRO staff was a featured speaker. All but one or two organizers completely avoided the platform where the leaders were seated throughout the
rally.)

While they looked for broad public recognition, the MWRO leaders also
appreciated the gratitude showed them by members whom they had helped with
an individual problem. Their satisfaction in having helped a fellow recipient was
intensified as those who had been helped reminded their friends of this fact.

Most of the satisfactions enjoyed by MWRO leaders are aspects of a single
underlying factor—that is, the repeated evidence that they were important not
powerless, that they had to be taken account of rather than taken for granted.
Through invitations to speaking engagements and offers of seats on the boards
of directors of voluntary associations, the leaders received proof that others
considered their opinions to be important, that they were respected members
of the community.

In short, the MWRO provided a vehicle for its lay leaders to use the civil
rights slogan first popularized by the Rev. Dr. Martin Luther King, Jr.: "I am

somebody." MWRO organizers who sometimes wondered what they were
accomplishing besides getting furniture for women found it particularly satisfying to see a previously shy and inarticulate lay leader of a local affiliate walk
nervously to the witness stand during a public hearing and then proudly
announce to the assembled legislators, officials, and others in the audience,
*"I am Louise _____, chairman of the Pilgrim City Welfare Rights Organ-
ization."* Because of the MWRO, she *was* somebody.

Despite their personal satisfaction, many MWRO lay leaders complained
that they were being "used" by the organization and constantly threatened
to resign. However, since these leaders received a formidable array of benefits
from the staff in return for the time they devoted to the organization, one
might objectively argue that the arrangement was reciprocal—each needed to
use the other as a means for desired ends.

Nevertheless, the real importance of the various sources of satisfactions
to MWRO leaders was underlined by the ferocity of their efforts to remain in
office whenever challenged. In much the same manner as labor union officials,
most MWRO lay leaders dreaded the possibility of ever having to "return to
the ranks."[5] Those leaders who were unable to stave off defeat almost always
severed all connections with the organization rather than accept a minor role.
The attempts of the MWRO statewide leaders to postpone the convention at
which they would face re-election and their subsequent refusal to admit defeat
after that convention, as discussed in earlier chapters, represent the clearest
example of this phenomenon.

The Lay Leaders: Bridge between Members and Staff

The differences in priorities between the MWRO organizers and the general
membership have been discussed in previous chapters; the former was primarily
concerned with increasing the power of poor people by organizing them while
the latter was concerned almost exclusively with ways for maximizing income
from the Welfare Department. As was shown in Table 5-2, the MWRO staff
gave the goal "Getting goods for mothers" the lowest rating of 11 possible
goals listed in the interview schedule. Yet, 38 of 44 staff members who were
interviewed indicated that they felt that the typical MWRO member would
give the highest rating to "getting the goods."

The MWRO lay leadership did not agree wholeheartedly with either of these
two positions. Because of their close contact with organizers and perhaps
because their life experience differed from that of many of the members, the
MWRO lay leadership often took positions between the two extremes. These
leaders neither thought nor acted like the general membership or the staff.
Instead they served as a bridge between the two, and as was suggested earlier

their ability to play this role of middle-man was a major factor in determining the ability of the MWRO to carry out organizing drives and to maintain the groups created in those drives.

The relationships between the organizational priorities of the MWRO organizers, lay leaders, and general members is summarized in Table 6-1. The role of the lay leader as middle-man is strikingly illustrated with respect to the goals most directly relevant to the basic orientations of the staff and members respectively. (For a discussion of differences in attitudes and priorities within other organizations, see Herbert McClosky's study of political parties,[6] and that of Luttberg and Ziegler on the Oregon Teachers Association.[7] Neither study makes the three-way distinction between organizer, leader, and member, however.)

The MWRO leadership sample saw themselves as only slightly less interested in the receipt of material benefits than was the general membership, but both leaders' and members' views on this subject were at wide variance with those of the organizers. On the other hand, the leadership views on the goal of building the power of the poor were virtually identical to those of the organizing staff; both organizers and leaders gave this goal a considerably higher priority than they imagined the typical member would.

The differences between organizers and leaders over the inherent value of distributing supplementary welfare grants for their own sake (as opposed to serving as an organizing tool) led to some conflict between the two. The MWRO staff felt that benefits should be distributed only to those who were making active contributions to local group activity. From their point of view, the "professional" organizer should not be concerned with helping people or making their lives more pleasant unless these activities also lead to a strengthening of the organization and hence further power to the poor. Without a redistribution of power, they felt, all efforts to resolve individual grievances would not make a dent in the operations of the Welfare Department and other major institutions of society. With such a redistribution, most of the causes for individual grievances would disappear. As was so often the case, the point of view of the MWRO staff was similar to a position put forward by Saul Alinsky. According to Alinsky, he could think of no higher form of "social treason" than to help people get adjusted so that they will "live in hell and like it too."[8]

Despite this attitude on the part of the staff, however, a majority of the leaders indicated that they opposed limiting benefits and grievance work to dues-paying members. They were either unaware of the principle that restricting service to active members could be used to strengthen their groups or they felt that the need to so strengthen their groups was outweighed by the desirability of helping a fellow welfare recipient mother who was faced with a major problem. MWRO lay leaders often distributed furniture or clothing request forms to women who merely promised to join the organization at some future

Table 6-1
Ratings Given to Organizational Goals[a]

	Staff	Lay Leaders	General Membership as estimated by	
			Staff	Leaders
A. Getting goods for the mothers[b]	2.6	4.5	4.8	4.9
B. Politicizing the mothers	4.5	4.3	2.0	2.3
C. Building strong local groups	4.2	4.7	3.6	4.0
D. Building a strong statewide organization	4.1	4.7	2.8	3.4
E. Building a strong national organization	4.1	4.4	2.3	2.7
F. Building the power of the poor	4.7	4.7	3.5	3.5
G. Building middle class support	2.9	3.9	2.3	3.3
H. Laying the groundwork for the "revolution"	3.3	3.8	1.3	3.1
I. Gaining adequate income	3.9	4.7	4.3	4.7
J. Training non-recipients in organizing	3.6	3.4	1.5	2.8
K. Leadership training to eventually eliminate the need for non-recipient organizers	3.1	3.1	2.8	2.8

[a]The numbers given in each cell represent the mean ratings given by those in that category for that goal. Respondents were all asked to rate the importance of these goals from 1 (low) to 5 (high) for themselves and, in their opinion, for the general membership.

[b]The exact wording of goals differed in some cases between the staff and leadership questionnaires.

point. However, it should not be overlooked that a substantial minority of the leaders did agree with the position of the MWRO staff on this issue, which points to their role as a bridge.

The MWRO lay leadership served as middle-men between the organizers and the membership not only on the issue of the need to redistribute power but also on the necessity to build poor people's organizations to do so. Both the staff and lay leaders gave the goals of building strong local, statewide, and national organizations a considerably higher rating than they imagined the members would have done.

Although the MWRO lay leaders virtually ignored the existence of a welfare rights movement outside of their state except at elections and times of crisis, they played an important role in familiarizing the membership with the concept of the national movement. National conventions and regional meetings of the National Welfare Rights Organization gave the lay leaders a chance to express their pride in their organization. Furthermore, before sending delegates to any such gathering, the lay chairman of the MWRO would warn them to be on their best behavior because "the reputation of Massachusetts is at stake."

The MWRO lay leadership varied greatly in political knowledge and sophistication; they spanned the spectrum between the largely uninformed general membership and the politically sensitive staff. Although all but one of the leaders interviewed were able to evaluate the job being done by Johnie Tillman, then the (lay) chairman of the National Welfare Rights Organization, only half of them could offer some opinion about Senator George McGovern, one of the Washington officials most sympathetic to welfare rights demands. Fewer than half of those in the sample could identify Roy Wilkins.

In view of the seemingly wide gaps in the political awareness of the MWRO lay leadership, it is impossible to generalize about the nature of their values or ideology, and it is difficult to say whether radical or moderate could more appropriately be applied. When one leader was asked to evaluate the importance of the goal "laying the groundwork for 'the revolution,' " she replied, "I really don't know what that means." Another responded that she had always considered herself a revolutionary. When pressed as to just what that term meant, she explained:

> By revolutionary, I mean that if we can't get change through the
> the system, I do believe we'll just have to break it up until we get it.

Few lay leaders, however, had a firm position on this possibility of gaining adequate income for poor people without a radical change in our system of government.

Despite the low level of information demonstrated by many MWRO lay leaders, they did assimilate a number of the basic political beliefs of the MWRO staff and helped carry them to the general membership. Every member of the leadership responded vehemently and negatively when asked to comment on the war in Vietnam. Almost all recognized that their own slogan of "$5500 or fight"—since raised to $6500—was only a slogan and that in fact an even higher amount was necessary for a family of four to live adequately in Massachusetts.

The MWRO lay leaders shared the staff's skepticism about the intentions of even those politicians who claimed to be friendly. When leaders were asked, "Do you think there are any politicians who are on the side of the welfare recipients today?" roughly three-fourths responded in the negative or were unable to name anyone. Two thought that there was a possibility that a few politicians might be depended upon to support their interests and only 3 answered in the affirmative. The 5 leaders who saw at least some possibility that some politicians might be on their side mentioned three United States Senators—Eugene McCarthy, sponsor of the NWRO Adequate Income Act of 1970, Edward Kennedy, and Birch Bayh—along with a state legislator and a member of the Boston City Council.

The MWRO lay leaders were aware of differences in priorities between themselves and both staff and members. Only one of the leaders in the sample saw her own position on the 11 organizational goals to be closer to those of the general membership than those of the staff. The lay leadership consensus was closer to the positions attributed to the staff than that attributed to the general membership for all but 2 of the 11 goals.

The MWRO lay leaders did side with the members rather than the staff on issues relating to the necessity of non-recipient organizers. Many demonstrated that they did not value the staff's efforts to build and maintain the organization and seemed to feel that the movement could get along quite well without non-recipient organizers—if only the recipients were more willing to devote additional time to organizational matters.

Two of the (white) MWRO lay leaders, however, who did not share the majority's view, nearly became organizers themselves. They took part in staff meetings, often tried to interpret the positions taken by the staff to the other lay leaders, and since they had become quite fluent in New Left rhetoric, used the same slang as did the staff. With the passage of time, they began to think in the staff's instrumental-directive manner—that is, for example, to plan whose car they would ride in to meetings according to who else might be in the car and in need of persuasion on certain issues. While the majority of lay leaders served as a bridge between staff and membership, these two played the more crucial role of providing a link between the staff and those other leaders.

7

Welfare Rights and the Study of Voluntary Associations

The history of the Massachusetts Welfare Rights Organization has a number of implications for the study of voluntary associations and interest group behavior. The first of these is a reiteration of the utility of the analytic framework based on incentives—the theory that asserts that organizational behavior can best be explained by analyzing the inducements offered to potential members and contributors. The MWRO, however, with its sharp differentiation in class background between organizers and general membership illustrates the need to modify incentive theory as it has thus far been presented to take into account the varying motivations of different organizational components.

The MWRO experience also shed further light on the issue of the degree to which the class background of the members affects an organization's structure and functioning. Although one must be wary of generalizations based on the study of a single organization, the organizational behavior of low-income groups seems to be based on the criterion of economic rationality; poor people act as if they were carefully calculating the economic effects of their actions.

Welfare Rights and the Incentive Theory of Organization

Peter B. Clark and James Q. Wilson have suggested that "organizations may be distinguished by the incentives [inducements to participate] upon which they principally rely" and that "analysis of several kinds of incentive systems can provide not only a way to classify much existing data about organizations, but also the rudiments of a predictive theory of organizational behavior."[1] Clark and Wilson describe three kinds of such incentives:

(a) Materials incentives: These are tangible rewards; that is, rewards that have a monetary value or can easily be translated into ones that have. . . .

(b) Solidary incentives: Solidary rewards are basically intangible; that is, the reward has no monetary value and cannot easily be translated into one that has. . . . They derive in the main from the act of associating. . . . Their common characteristics is that they tend to be independent of the precise ends of the association. . . .

113

(c) Purposive incentives: Purposive, like solidary, incentives are intangible, but they derive in the main from the stated goals of the association rather than from the simple act of associating.[2]

Although this incentive theory was first advanced before the welfare rights movement came into existence, a number of the authors' hypotheses were born out by MWRO activities. The major attraction of the MWRO for its members was the receipt of supplementary welfare payments in the form of special needs grants; the MWRO therefore can be described as dependent upon material incentives. Clark and Wilson noted that such organizations had a minimum of uncertainty as to goal achievement and that this in turn placed organizational executives "under greater pressure to 'produce.' "[3] This pressure played an important role in the evolution of the MWRO; it necessitated a modification by the staff of many of the New Left ideals as well as the displacement of goals from the building of stable pressure groups of poor people towards successive replication and perfection of the techniques involved in the Boston model organizing drives. (The MWRO also provides an excellent example of Phillip Selznick's generalization that "day-to-day behavior of the group becomes centered around specific problems and proximate goals that have primarily an internal relevance."[4] In organizations with material incentives and hence relatively clear performance measures, the proximate goals would in all likelihood be clearer and hence the pressures even stronger.)

The MWRO history also provides support for the Clark and Wilson contention that in organizations based on material inducements "stated purposes are not important incentives and have relatively little impact upon incentives."[5] The MWRO general membership was concerned almost exclusively with immediately realizable benefits; for them, the formal goals of the organization—building the power of the poor and achieving a guaranteed adequate income—were not very important. (The goal of building the power of the poor *was* of prime importance to the MWRO organizers, who were not responding primarily to material incentives.)

Incentive theory suggests the value of comparing welfare rights with other organizations that also depend primarily upon material benefits. The absence of racial rhetoric in the MWRO is somewhat parallel to the case of the late Congressman William Dawson's political machine, another organization offering tangible benefits and services to a population similar to that of the MWRO.

The Dawson organization, like the MWRO, depended upon its ability to "deliver" tangible benefits and thus had no need for expressive issues. Former Congressman Adam Clayton Powell, on the other hand, had little of a tangible nature to distribute to his followers and so he, like a number of black community organization leaders who could not provide tangible benefits, was constrained to rely on a heavy diet of racial rhetoric and other expressive issues.

The Dawson machine gave up appeals to race issues as soon as it was in a position to distribute tangible benefits. The MWRO staff was in a position to distribute such benefits from the start and thus had no need for (and being white could not easily provide) racial rhetoric. In view of the nature and attitudes of the constituency and the ability to continue producing benefits, the ability to "deliver" in both cases made the organizations largely immune to challenges based on race or ideology.

The MWRO also shared with other organizations dependent upon material incentives the need to struggle continually to attract new resources; this resulted from the fact that a benefit already distributed no longer sufficed to promote participation. Just as the employee of a business firm would quit just as soon as the firm could no longer provide paychecks, the MWRO membership was ready to quit as soon as the special needs grants stopped. The difficulties encountered by the MWRO in motivating participation once benefits had been distributed directly paralleled those faced by the Philadelphia-based Consumers Educational and Protectional Association (CEPA), which sought to involve consumers in helping each other fight businesses involved in unfair practices. CEPA members, like MWRO members, proved unwilling to help others in picketting stores once their own grievances were settled. CEPA restricted its assistance to dues-paying members who formally pledged to take comparable action to help others with their grievances in the future, but it too appeared to be plagued by members drifting away after their initial receipt of benefits.[6]

Despite the basic utility of their formulations, several Clark and Wilson hypotheses appear in need of modification in the light of the MWRO case study. For example, the authors speculate that organizations that depend upon tangible incentives

> . . . will be highly flexible about their activities. Activities may change without disrupting member participation as long as material incentives continue to be available. . . . Such organizations will also be tactically flexible to the extent that tactical shifts do not interfere with their income of incentive resources.[7]

The MWRO organizers quickly developed a standard operating procedure, which members came to expect, that limited their flexibility to adopt new tactics that did not involve a mass demonstration followed by filing benefit request forms. Another limitation, especially powerful for poor people's organizations, is the lack of alternative sources of resources. The success of the welfare rights movement derived in large measure from its discovery of a relatively cost-free source of benefits, the supplementary welfare checks for special needs grants. The MWRO was unable to find equivalent sources of benefits and its flexibility was severely limited—and remained that way until alternative sources were discovered or the response of the membership to incentives change in some manner.

Clark and Wilson offer two further hypotheses both of which are also in
need of re-interpretation:

> Groups that produce or obtain few material or solidary incentives
> will be forced to rely mainly upon purposes; for example, voluntary
> associations composed of very poor or low status members. . . . During
> their formative stages, most groups will rely heavily upon purposes as
> incentives.[8]

The MWRO staff was able to overcome the handicaps of lower-class membership
and newness of their organization by discovering and exploiting a loophole in
the institutional structure of a target institution. The case of the MWRO thus
suggests that the underlying variable in both hypotheses should be the availability
of material benefits rather than either the socio-economic status of the general
membership or the age of the organization. If similar loopholes could be found
in the benefit disbursement procedures of other institutions, it would not be
surprising to see the emergence of new organizations that base their appeal on
the receipt of material benefits.

Most importantly, the Clark–Wilson formulation is limited by its focus on
only the primary incentive system for an organization. A more complete formulation would require paying attention to the major components of the organization and the different incentives to which personnel in each component
respond. Different individuals in an organization often respond to different
incentives; if these individuals belong to different organizational components,
the activity of the organization as a whole can best be explained by the interaction of the varying requirements imposed by the different incentive systems
in each component.

In the welfare rights movement, important differences in motivation arose
out of the differences in background between the organizers and the welfare
recipients who made up the general membership. The lack of organizational
experience and the low level of organizational activity of the general membership made the gap in perspective between organizers and members particularly
obvious in this case, but similar differences can undoubtedly be found in other
organizations as well. Studies have already demonstrated this to be true for
those at various levels in political party organizations,[9] an interest group of
teachers,[10] and in organizations involved in the foreign policy-making process.[11]

The importance of considering organizational components separately and
then analyzing the incentives for each of them can be illustrated by considering the misperceptions that arise from a failure to do so. Gilbert Steiner's
discussion of the National Welfare Rights Organization in *The State of Welfare*
suffers from a number of these failings. For example, Steiner has written:

> NWRO's history and style thus lead support to the proposition
> that formal organizations have certain unfailing characteristics whether

they are businessmen in Rotary Clubs, undergraduates in fraternities, physicians in medical associations, or welfare mothers in NWRO. The latter now has a written constitution, an annual convention, a regular publication. It sells its own distinctive jewelry and its own note-paper. . . .

[George] Wiley wants a self-sufficient, dues-supported organization that will not depend on churches, unions, or the poverty program. He believes that the way to reach this goal is to make the NWRO attractive to its potential constituency—by emphasizing a unique, shared exper-ience, and by building in the trappings and techniques of middle-class organizations that Americans are apt to join. Welfare clients, in other words, are attracted by an opportunity to do the things that other, more affluent persons do and simultaneously to reinforce each other in efforts to better their condition.[12]

Our analysis of the history and development of the MWRO suggests that Steiner was misinformed on several scores. He failed to distinguish between the desires of Wiley and the organizers on the one hand and the general mem-bership on the other, or between the local lay leadership and the highly sophisticated women who led the statewide affiliates and who held national office. The middle-class trappings of organizational procedure were pressed by the staff and were a source of satisfaction for only a few lay leaders who made up an extremely small proportion of the total membership, which in turn was only a fraction of the total number of welfare recipients in this country. Far from enjoying elaborate parliamentary maneuvering, the typical MWRO member sought to avoid it and attended local group meetings if, and only if, there was some prospect of a tangible award attached to her attendance. Many organizations have depended upon solidary incentives to attract members to meetings and other activities, but the role of these incentives for the MWRO was limited except for a minority of the members and except for those affiliates in the more isolated and rural communities. Local welfare rights meetings were little more than informational transactions between member and either organizer or lay leader; they were not generally social gatherings.

In particular, Steiner failed to appreciate the significance of the strong input from the middle-class welfare rights staff into all aspects of organizational activity. The written constitution, conventions, and regular publications were in large part the result of policies favored by the organizers (and a small group of sophisticated lay leaders) who were concerned with building a conventional organization. The membership (and to a lesser extent, many lay leaders) appeared to have little concern in this area. Some MWRO lay leaders referred to their bylaws as an "organizers' document," which they believed had been drafted by staff members and lawyers. (It was in fact a jointly drafted docu-ment ratified at an MWRO convention.) MWRO members could be induced to attend annual conventions only when considerable side benefits were introduced.

The MWRO newspaper *The Adequate Income Times* had its major impetus from
the MWRO staff; it proved difficult to convince most local group lay leaders to
submit even a single paragraph of news on welfare rights activities in their
neighborhood.

Once introduced to the trappings of formal organization by the staff, some
welfare recipients did come to derive some satisfaction from them and began to
play an increasingly influential role in the movement activities. There are indications that this group of leaders was not typical of the general membership, however, and in any event, it is risky to generalize about the welfare rights movement from this small group of leaders with whom outsiders have had the most
contact.

The distribution of influence between organizers and lay leaders in the
planning and execution of organizational activities varied from local group to
local group throughout the country and within groups over the passage of time.
But it seems safe to say that the majority of the "unfailing characteristics"
that Steiner attributes to all organizations were due primarily to the influence
of welfare rights staff members and not related to any of the characteristics of
the welfare recipients in the general membership. Further support for this
understanding can be found by comparing the structure of the MWRO with
that of its welfare rights predecessor in Massachusetts, the Mothers for Adequate
Welfare (MAW). Although both groups' membership consisted of welfare recipients, the MWRO developed a complex structure while the MAWs did not. This
can be explained by the fact that Bill Pastreich had already determined what
kind of organization he wanted to create before he had ever set foot in Massachusetts while

> . . . MAW in its structure, activities, and goals embodied all of the anti-
> organizational biases of the SDS students who conceived and helped
> create it. It became an organization in the summer of 1965 without
> formulating bylaws, a constitution, electing officers, or seeking incor-
> poration under the laws of Massachusetts.[13]

In both cases, the structures reflected the proclivities of the organizers and not
the presumably constant attitudes of the welfare recipient population in Massachusetts.

In sum, Steiner's failure to consider the differing motivations of the various
components of the welfare rights movement obscured his view of its dynamics.
While he viewed the NWRO as based on solidary and purposive incentives that
provided "mutual reinforcement for a depressed social and economic group"
and for "participant representation in policy discussions independent of social
workers or other surrogate spokesmen" as well as "an associational tie for AFDC
than [sic] can be their equivalent of the League of Women Voters or Planned
Parenthood,"[14] the grassroots strength of the organization was really based upon
the lure of tangible benefits.

Without the perspective based on the analysis of the incentive system for each organizational component, it would have been impossible to explain the MWRO's record of highly successful organizing drives followed by a slow decline in local affiliates. Once that perspective is adopted, both aspects of the MWRO history can be easily understood. The organizing drives succeeded because the Boston model was designed to meet the disparate needs of organizers to build groups, members to gain benefits, and emerging lay leaders to gain their initial desires for respect and prominence. With the passage of time, however, the activities required to meet the needs of the three components became divergent; for example, when the staff sought further expansion of the MWRO, elements in the lay leadership opposed it. Viewed in this light, the failure of the MWRO was its inability to develop further program material to meet the divergent needs of its components. It is an open question whether any such program material could ever have been developed at all.

Welfare Rights and the Class Basis
of Organizations

According to conventional wisdom, Americans are a "nation of joiners" and the way to bring about change in society is to organize a group to do the lobbying. As Lee Rainwater puts it:

> If the most spontaneous American solution to any problem is to "pass a law," the second most popular solution is to "form an organization."[15]

Robert Dahl defines the "normal" American political process as "one in which there is a high probability that an active and legitimate group can make itself heard effectively at some crucial stage in the process of decision," a situation in which

> . . . one or more officials are not only ready to listen to the noise, but expect to suffer in some significant way if they do not placate the group, its leaders, or its most vociferous members.[16]

Many elements of this image of the American political process are open to question. Surveys of organizational affiliation have shown widely varying results although the preponderance of evidence gives some support to the "nation-of-joiners" thesis.[17] It is doubtful, however, whether the organizations to which most Americans belong have been organized to deal with the pressing personal problems facing the membership. Again quoting Rainwater:

> Organizations, including a great many political organizations prob-
> ably function more as entertainment and leisure-time activities than
> as serious mechanisms for attaining one's central life goals. Even organ-
> izations like the American Legion are, for the vast majority of their
> members, sources of entertainment, of a sense of belongingness and
> ideological indulgence rather than a major avenue to the solution of
> the problems of adaptation.[18]

Regardless of the appropriateness of this conventional wisdom for the
American public as a whole, there is little doubt that the lower classes have
faced major obstacles in organizing to further their interests. Social scientists
have reported that those of lower socio-economic status participate in voluntary associations at a lower rate than those of higher status and that the difficulties which poor people's groups face even after they have been organized to
the point of holding a few meetings.[19]

With few exceptions, those comparing the middle and lower classes have
stressed the greater obstacles in organizing the latter group. Lee Rainwater
has, for example, noted the greater difficulties that result from organizing
those holding low social status because joining an organization might be
viewed as associating oneself with a status from which one hopes to escape
in the near future.[20] This problem was sometimes encountered by MWRO
doorknockers who found considerable reluctance among women to admit
publicly that they were welfare recipients.

Rainwater further hypothesizes—and the experience of the MWRO tends
to confirm—that much of the previous contact with organizations by the poor
and other lower-class people has been negative. Much of the suspicion with
which MWRO doorknockers were greeted can be explained by Rainwater's
contention:

> To the extent that lower-class people have had experience with
> organization, that experience tends to make them not at all sanguine
> about the likelihood of rewards of participation. . . . Lower-class
> people expect to be manipulated, looked down upon, and exploited
> by organizations.[21]

Rainwater also provides a persuasive analysis of the often heard complaints
about the apathy among the lower social classes. Many of these complaints
result, he says, from organizers' misperceptions about the situation and needs
of the potential membership, the failure of the lower classes to view organization as a potential solution to their problems, and the fact that "so much
energy available to lower-class people is taken up in day-to-day survival that
there is little left over for organization."[22]

Somewhat surprisingly, if the experience of the MWRO can be taken as typical, the lower classes appear to show a good deal more economic rationality about their decision to participate in voluntary organizations than do many of those in the middle classes. In the case of the MWRO, the general membership demonstrated that they were carefully calculating the economic impact of all possible degrees of participation in voluntary associations by taking part only when there was a realistic prospect of a tangible return in the short run that could not be otherwise obtained.

The rule-of-thumb followed by welfare mothers in their relationship with the MWRO was that described by Mancur Olson in *The Logic of Collective Action*; namely, since they would probably benefit from the attainment of organizational goals whether or not they joined, it would be (economically) irrational to join:

> If the members of a large group rationally seek to maximize their personal welfare, they will *not* act to advance their common or group objectives unless there is coercion to force them to do so, or unless there is some separate incentive, distinct from the achievement of the common or group interest is offered to the members of the group individually on the condition that they help beat the costs or burdens involved in the achievement of group objectives.[23]

Olson's logic seems impeccable, and so we are forced to grapple with the issue of why it is apparently ignored by millions of members of American voluntary associations—unless of course they have joined these groups solely for the receipt of such "selective benefits" as newsletters, charter flights, and group life insurance—but not by welfare recipients.

Without economic rationality on the part of the poor, the MWRO organizers would have been free to stress the goals of lobbying to promote the interest of all welfare recipients, the goals of "adequate income, dignity, justice, and democracy" that appear prominently on much of the literature of the NWRO. As it was, the MWRO staff was forced to demonstrate continually that benefits could be guaranteed only to dues-paying members. They did this through an organizational monopoly of the request forms for benefits, and of the bargaining power to force acceptance of the requests.

Two explanations can be advanced for this apparent *greater* sensitivity of the poor to the dictates of economic rationality. The first involves the supply of resources available to be contributed to voluntary associations. The poor have little in the way of free time or money to contribute to organizational activities, according to this point of view, because virtually all of their resources are involved in the everyday struggle to survive. Therefore, whatever contributions the poor are called upon to make are relatively more expensive from their perspective and would be subject to greater scrutiny; the poor person would be less likely to pay the $10-a-year membership fees for some group without first calculating just what this expenditure might bring in return.

In a more speculative vein, the differential displays of economic rationality by different social classes can be associated with the theories of the "hierarchies of man's needs" advanced by Abraham Maslow[24] and Douglas McGregor.[25] According to Maslow, there are five levels of needs, in ascending order: (1) physiological, (2) safety needs including security, stability, and freedom from fear, (3) belongingness and love needs, (4) esteem needs, and (5) the need for self-actualization.[26] Both Maslow and McGregor argue that a satisfied need is not a motivator of human behavior and thus the prime motivating factors are those which derive from the level directly above the last satisfied need.

The Maslow–McGregor framework becomes directly relevant if one views poor people as still struggling to meet their physiological and safety needs (sometimes literally, always relatively as compared to the situation perceived to be true of other groups in society).

The higher levels of need in the Maslow–McGregor hierarchy do not meet Olson's criterion of rationality but are relevant to those who feel secure about their physiological and basic safety needs. For these reasons, we would not expect the Clark–Wilson solidary incentives to be attractive to poor people, or in Maslow's words:

> Higher needs require better outside conditions to make them possible. Better environmental conditions (familial, economic, political, educational, etc.) are all necessary to allow people to love each other rather than merely to keep them from killing each other.[27]

For welfare recipients, however, the environment is relatively hostile and they are forced to focus their attention upon the lowest level of needs, the needs for which Olson's formulations are most relevant.

In sum, the middle classes have already (presumably) satisfied their most pressing needs for food, shelter, and a measure of security through avenues other than voluntary associations. It should not therefore be surprising to see middle-class individuals turning to voluntary associations for the gratification of "higher needs" for which economic rationality is not relevant. It is not that *even* middle-class organizations are relatively unconcerned with basic needs and values, but that middle-class organizations *in particular* are involved with peripheral concerns. The reason there are not more organizations with a lower-class membership that concentrate on meeting the immediate and tangible needs of these people is not the lack of receptivity to such incentives but rather the difficulty in gaining sufficient resources to provide them.

These considerations lead to the following conclusion or, more precisely, a hypothesis in need of empirical validation:

> Large numbers of poor people can be induced to join voluntary associations, but only in a very restricted set of circumstances. In particular, participation can be elicited in return for the credible promise of benefits that have a concrete impact upon the lives of the members. The major barrier to the organization of the poor has thus been that few of those who have tried to accomplish this have been able to offer the required incentives.

The MWRO was able to exploit a loophole in the Welfare Department regulations that enabled it to offer supplementary welfare checks to dues-paying members and thus appealed to those who acted as if they were following Mancur Olson's concept of economic rationality. To the extent that other groups could discover similar tangible benefits that could be tied to participation in organizational activities, one would expect them to be equally successful.

This hypothesis is consistent with many of the previously stated propositions concerning organizing the poor—propositions that can now be viewed as special cases of our general hypothesis. Thus for example, Saul Alinsky has suggested that the key to community organizing is through the expression of hostility and conflict:

> The community organizer digs into the morass of resignation, hopelessness, and despair and works with local people in articulating (or "rubbing raw") their resentments. . . . When those prominent in the status quo call you an agitator, they are completely correct, that is, in one word, your function—to agitate to the point of conflict.[28]

The history of the MWRO suggests that agitation is not a necessary ingredient in eliciting initial participation. What is necessary is the concreteness and personal impact that conflict situations usually engender. On the other hand, the experience of those welfare rights groups that did not develop any hostility towards their caseworkers suggests that conflict may be necessary to preserve a feeling of militancy over time. Had the MWRO staff been able to maintain a steady flow of benefits, they might have maintained the functioning of their organization. But without some hostility towards caseworkers and other government officials, it is unlikely that they could have continued winning the confrontations that made those benefits available.

James Q. Wilson has suggested that

> . . . except for organizations which are in some sense extensions of the family and the church, lower-income neighborhoods are more likely to produce collective action in response to threats (real or imagined) than to create opportunities.[29]

If this is true, it can be attributed to the greater concreteness and immediacy attached to threats as opposed to the vague promises—usually advanced by community organizers—that concern some better living standard by sometime in the future. (For example, "join our group and help fight airport expansion and reduce the noise from jet planes.") In Wilson's words:

> They [lower classes] are likely to collaborate when each person can see a danger to him or his family in some proposed change: collective action is a way not of defining and implementing some broad program for the benefit of all, but of giving force to individual objections by adding them together in collective protest.[30]

During MWRO confrontations in welfare offices, it was individual desire for benefits rather than individual objections that were being aggregated, but the process was the same.

These considerations concerning the motives of the poor should go a long way in explaining class differences in voluntary associational activity, but the impact of non-attitudinal factors can not be ignored. In general, the middle classes have more resources to contribute to their organizations, more standing in the community to win a hearing for their grievances, and problems that are less central to their daily existence. One would expect groups with a middle-class base to seek fewer far-reaching changes in society—if not merely the retention of the status quo. Thus, even with attitudinal factors held constant, one would expect that those groups with a middle- (and of course upper-) class membership would find it easier to recruit members, maintain themselves, and to demonstrate progress towards achievement of their goals. In conclusion, we adopt Lee Rainwater's judgment that because of the overwhelming problems facing the poor

> It is possible that if lower class people were as skilled and as ready for organization as the middle classes are believed to be, they would still not be able to achieve their goals by organizational action.[31]

8 Toward a Theory of Protest

The theoretical framework for our understanding of protest activity builds upon the foundations laid in the works of James Q. Wilson[1] and Michael Lipsky.[2] Both describe protest as the process by which relatively powerless or excluded groups (henceforth called "protest groups") seek concessions from others (henceforth "the target") without starting with any positive compensations to offer in return. Their formulations differ, however, in that Wilson's focuses upon efforts to enter into a direct bargaining relationship between protest group and target, while Lipsky's focuses upon the efforts of protest groups to activate third parties to enter the fray.

According to Wilson, protest is to be distinguished from bargaining in that the former depends upon the "exclusive use of negative inducements (threats) that rely, for their effect, on sanctions which require mass action and response."[3] In other words, a group with nothing positive to offer can still threaten harm. This paradigm emphasizes direct confrontation (or at least the threat of direct confrontation) between protest group and target; the need for intermediaries is minimized. Examples of this "protest as confrontation" include picketting, sit-down strikes, and boycotts—or at least the threat of these actions.

Although Lipsky accepts the utility of the bargaining framework to analyze protest group activity, he explicitly rejects the "simplistic pressure group model which would posit a direct relationship between pressure group and pressured" because "the essence of political protest consists of activating third parties to participate in controversy in ways favorable to protest goals."[4]

Examples of this "protest as showmanship" paradigm include lunch counter sit-ins in the South in the early 1960s and other civil rights activities of that era aimed primarily at winning the support of Northern liberals. As is shown in Figure 8-1, Lipsky's paradigm includes four major elements: the protest group ("A") and target institution ("B") that are the only elements necessary to describe protest as confrontation, as well as a reference public ("C") that the protest group seeks to activate in order to put pressure on the target, and the communications media ("D") through which the protest group hopes to transmit its message.

The Wilson and Lipsky formulations should be seen as special cases of a more general theory of protest. In this more general theory, protest refers to public collective activities intended to promote modification or abandonment of policies in a context in which the target is powerful enough to ignore those seeking the concessions. Efforts to force targets to the bargaining table by

Figure 8-1. Protest as Showmanship[a] (With Example of Rent Strikers)

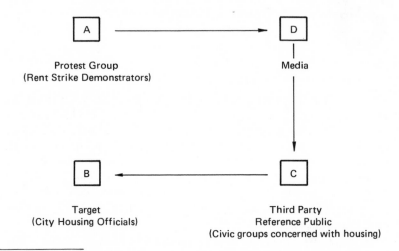

[a]This is a simplified version of Lipsky's paradigm excluding multiple actors and feed-back effects. The complete Lipsky paradigm can be found in "Protest as a Political Resource," p. 1147.

groups that lack positive compensations to offer thus lie at the heart of all pro-test activity.

A given protest activity, as defined above, can be thought of as falling primarily into one of three major modes: confrontation, showmanship, or organizational aggrandizement. Each of the three is characterized by a different relationship of the protest group and other actors; each serves a different pur-pose. The first two modes—protest as confrontation and protest as showman-ship—are simply the Wilson and Lipsky paradigms as already discussed. The third—protest as organizational aggrandizement—includes a whole range of activities that have not always been considered in the same context as the first two.

Protest as organizational aggrandizement includes those protest activities aimed at strengthening the group for future protest activities. Organizational aggrandizement typically works as follows: by staging events that attract the attention of the media, the leader of a protest organization increases the visi-bility of his group and, hopefully, its reputed potency. This in turn strengthens the leader's ability to threaten the target in future confrontation or to activate third parties to intervene. Media coverage of protest group activities can also be useful in demonstrating organizational strength to members (and potential members) of the group to promote their future participation and to financial supporters (and potential supporters) to promote their future contributions.

Events staged primarily to impress the mass media with the newsworthiness of group activities, and hence to promote future media coverage of the group, could also be viewed as organizational aggrandizement

Lipsky introduces the term "community organization" to describe those activities designed to "increase the relative cohesion of groups or to increase the perception of group solidarity as a precondition to greater cohesion."[5] Some such activities—mass meetings for example—meet the definition of protest presented above and can constitute the "organizational aggrandizement" mode of protest. Other community organization activities—such as mailing fund-raising materials or conducting door-to-door membership drives—do not involve public collective activity and would therefore be excluded from our definition of protest. Our term "organizational aggrandizement" and Lipsky's "community organization" overlap to a considerable extent but are distinct conceptually.

Protest as organizational aggrandizement can thus be employed to promote future successes in showmanship or confrontation—or even traditional bargaining—if enough resources can be accumulated. Examples of protest as organizational aggrandizement include the MWRO rally held on the Boston Common to celebrate the third birthday of the welfare rights movement. Using the same symbols employed earlier, three versions of the aggrandizement paradigm are illustrated below in Figures 8-2, 8-3, and 8-4.

As is evident from our discussion of the three modes of protest, organized group activity is necessary in all three of them. They differ, however, in their involvement of media, third parties, and target. Confrontation requires only protest group and target; showmanship involves four different elements: a group using the media to activate third parties which in turn can put pressure on the target. Organizational aggrandizement involves both the protest group and (normally) the media but may be intended to impress the target, potential financial supporters, potential coalition partners, media executives or even the protest group members and potential members themselves.

The history of the MWRO indicates that all three modes of protest have been used virtually simultaneously by the same organization. From this we derive the conclusion that the three modes of protest may be most profitably understood as *options* available to (the leader of) a protest group in seeking to advance organizational ends in a given context.

The selection of an appropriate mode of protest depends upon a broad range of factors that collectively determine the likelihood of success with a given level of resources, and hence the context of the activity. Simply put, the appropriate mode is the one most likely to lead to a victory in a given context.

Organizational maintenance needs are themselves one of four major determinants of the optimum mode of protest group action. The nature of the target institution is a second important determinant: what, for example, is its structure

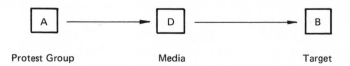

Figure 8-2. Protest as Organizational Aggrandizement (Target-Oriented)

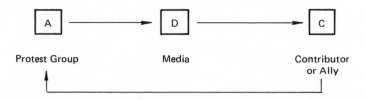

Figure 8-3. Protest as Organizational Aggrandizement (Contributor-or Ally-Oriented)

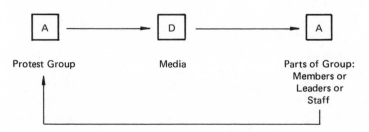

Figure 8-4. Protest as Organizational Aggrandizement (Internally Oriented)

and its experience in dealing with protest group activities? The nature of the political system in which the group is operating is a third important factor. Are there, for example, many potentially sympathetic third parties which could be activiated to intervene in a manner favorable to the protest group? How accepting will the general public—and its representatives in law enforcement agencies—be towards particular disruptive tactics? Finally, there are a whole series of factors relating to the personal knowledge, interests, skills, proclivities, and organizing (or political) philosophy of the group's staff and/or lay leaders. To what degree, for example, are the staff/leaders willing to engage in the tedious efforts that are necessary to build a grassroots organization? To what degree do they believe that formal organization is needed to achieve their policy objectives at all?

The first three sets of factors—maintenance needs, target, and setting—determine the likelihood of success of a given tactic (mode of protest) for a group. The fourth set allows for idiosyncratic departures from perfect rationality—lack of information, for example—as well as possible divergences from an identity of purpose between the needs of the leadership and the needs of the group. In other words, one could substantially account for group activities by a careful analysis of the first three sets of factors, but uncertainty would always remain due to the idiosyncratic factors.

The discussion to this point can be summarized in the following basic propositions:

1. There are at least three modes of protest group activity, each with its own distinctive relationship between protest group, target, third parties, and media, and each serves a distinctive purpose.[a]

2. The theoretical framework for the analysis of protest group activity must therefore go beyond consideration of the internal dynamics of the protest organization and its interaction with the target institution. In particular, it should take account of the four elements introduced in Lipsky's paradigm and listed above.

3. The crucial building blocks of the theoretical framework should be a series of hypotheses outlining the specific circumstances that call for (or suggest to the fully rational protest group leader) a given mode of protest and hence a specific configuration of the four elements.

4. The hypotheses concerning the choice of modes of protest by group decision-makers can best be organized by grouping them into four sets of factors: (a) the organizational maintenance needs of the protest group—including its current ability to command resources, (b) the nature of the target institution, (c) the general political setting in which the group is operating, and (d) a residual category of factors relating to the particular characteristics of the protest group decision-makers themselves.

By considering each of the four sets of factors in turn, one can derive a series of hypotheses that, when taken together, should explain the choice of

---

[a]It should be recognized that these three modes represent ideal types. In reality, protest activity generally serves all three purposes to a greater or lesser extent. In those cases in which the protest group is attempting to engage in direct confrontation with its target, the leaders of the target institution must still make their responses in the face of potential reaction on the part of superiors in their own organization and of those in reference publics. How for example will the constituencies of the target institution respond to what may appear to be abandonment of principles in response to lawless threats?[6] On the other hand, one would expect that the target of protest as showmanship would still take note of the protest group activity and perhaps even consider possible responses without (or before) the pressure which can be exerted by activated third parties. In addition to this, well publicized confrontation or showmanship can serve the purposes of aggrandizement, and aggrandizement activities can result in the activation of third parties or perhaps even put direct pressure on targets themselves.

modes of protest. (Although our discussion treats each of the four sets of factors primarily as independent variables, they are obviously interrelated. A more fully elaborated theoretical framework would spell out the interaction of the factors in detail.)

The organizational maintenance needs of the protest group are probably the most important factor in determining the modes of protest to be employed. These needs fall into two main categories. First, what must be done in order to promote continued participation by existing members and/or the attraction of new ones? Secondly, what must be done in order to maintain the supply of resources which are necessary to carry out those activities which prompt the membership participation?

One of the key variables in this regard is the members' (or the organizers' or the contributors') need for tangible evidence of organizational effectiveness. To the extent that symbolic victories will suffice in the short run, it is possible to satisfy members with protest as showmanship. But if the members of the group will not wait for legislation to be drafted, lobbied for, enacted, and then administered, protest group leadership will be constrained to engage in confrontation with targets which can provide more or less immediate benefits.

The ability to succeed in confrontation is normally increased as the number of participants increases. But the relationship between available resources and preferred modes of protest is more complex than this statement would suggest. Thus to the extent that organizational maintenance requires goods that can be won only through confrontation, this creates a need to retain the capacity to mobilize a large proportion of the general membership for protest activities. Accordingly, reliance upon confrontation may entail a much higher demand for organizational resources to prompt membership activity than would be required for either showmanship or aggrandizement.

On the other hand, members who would be satisfied with symbolic achievements by the group, and hence by showmanship or aggrandizement, do not require the attention from leadership or the resources that the confrontation mode introduces. This serves to reinforce the bias towards showmanship or aggrandizement among those groups that are the weakest.

Lipsky's writings suggest another connection between available resources and mode of protest. If a group cannot muster the resources to engage in activity that harms—or at least creates discomfort in—the target institution, it must confine its efforts to showmanship and aggrandizement. It should be stressed, however, that there is no *absolute* threshold of bargaining resources for a given group, taken in isolation. Differences in the nature of the target institutions with which a group may interact can create situations in which the group is beyond the threshold of necessary resources, in one case, and hopelessly below it in others. In certain contexts, this threshold can be quite low. The threat of disruption, for example, requires only little in the way of physical resources. Thus a group lacking enough bargaining resources to cross the

required threshold in one context is forced to rely on showmanship or aggrandizement if it seeks to influence a particular target. But the group could, quite
conceivably, still be able to engage in coercive activities against some other
target and defer action against the first target until some later time when group
power (or at least reputed power) would be greater.

Three aspects of target institutions appear most important in determining
the appropriateness of various modes of protest. Perhaps the most crucial of
these is the degree of decentralization within the target institution, particularly
the discretion to disburse rewards. Closely related to this is the degree of
legitimacy with which protest group demands are viewed both within the target
institution and within its reference publics. One would expect confrontation
tactics to be most successful in those cases in which officials of the target
institution had a high degree of discretion to disburse awards and viewed the
demands as basically legitimate. In those cases in which discretion is limited
or non-existent and the demands are viewed as illegitimate, the protest group
is forced to seek modification of the rules or standard practices of the target,
which process often requires protracted negotiations during which membership
interest and hence coercive potential is likely to decline. In these cases, showmanship or aggrandizement would be the preferred modes of protest since
group power is unequal to the task of confrontation in that context.

The final important aspect of the target institution is its experience in
dealing with protest activity, especially with disruptive protest. The first
time a target is faced with a disruptive demonstration, its leadership would
in all likelihood be unsure of how to proceed; it might be likely to make
initial concessions in the hope that this would satisfy the militant groups.
When a target is surprised by the protesters, confusion and hence the likelihood of concessions would be even greater. For these reasons, one might
expect—and often finds—a "law of diminishing returns" with respect to confrontations directed against the same target.

On the other hand, one can conceive of a target which is both inexperienced and fiercely hostile to the protesters, that might react to disruptive activities with an inordinate amount of toughness: for example, Southern small
town police faced with their first civil rights demonstration. For this reason,
empirical research is required to delineate further the effect of such factors as
inexperience of the target.

The third determinant of the appropriateness of a given mode of protest
is the political setting. The response of third parties to protest group efforts
is particularly crucial. All forms of protest require a certain range of response
from the general public. Showmanship, if it is to be effective, generally
requires support for either the group or its goals from major segments of
society. Confrontation (and to a lesser extent aggrandizement) generally
requires public passivity, the absence of revulsion strong enough to prompt
(or justify) harsh repression of protest activities before the group is strong

enough to defend itself. Third party indifference can be fatal to showmanship but is desirable for confrontation. Thus the public attitudes that vary from community to community may rule out certain modes of protest in some locales and promote that mode of protest in others.

The possibility of a negative response to protest group activity either by the general public or by more specialized reference publics has not received appropriate stress in previous discussions of protest. Most of the cases discussed by Wilson and Lipsky, for example, were ones in which the dramatization of an issue would generally result in increased support from those third parties who would be most able to affect the target. This would appear to be the case both for civil rights demonstrators in the South who sought to activate Northern liberals and the New York City rent strikers who looked for support from many of these same elements.

For other groups, especially the heavily stigmatized, the avenue of protest as showmanship is not very promising. In cases in which third party support is either non-existent or extremely narrowly defined, exposure through the mass media may even be counterproductive. When support is narrowly defined, attempts to reach potential supporters through more specialized communications links as organizational newletters would be a far more effective way of proceeding.

In those contexts in which mass media exposure results in more opposition than support for the group and its goals, confrontation would appear to be the only mode of protest likely to further group ends—although some aggrandizement would probably be necessary from time to time, for internal purposes, to demonstrate organizational activity to members and contributors, whatever the effects on other third parties.

Another important aspect of the political setting is the legal framework under which the group is operating. In particular, confrontation is promoted in those localities and at those times in which the penalties for disruptive behavior are minimal and/or their enforcement lax. Enforcement of penalties for trespass and similar actions would in all likelihood be somewhat dependent upon the perceived legitimacy of the protest group demands by the community at large as well as by officials of the target and the law enforcement agencies.

The final set of determinants of the mode of protest to be employed consists of ideosyncratic factors such as the proclivities, priorities, and organizing philosophies of the organizers and/or leaders. One variable of this nature is the reaction of the organizer/leader to personal publicity. A leader who derives a good deal of personal satisfaction from seeing himself (and having others see himself) on television might be inclined to promote showmanship among his followers even when the perfectly rational leader with organizational maintenance needs in mind would pick another mode of protest.

Although the short-run considerations of a protest group leader include both strengthening his organization and bringing about a situation that is conducive to the kind of change he favors, the relative weight given to these two broad goals varies from individual to individual and from group to group. The relative priority given to these two goals—which we call "organizational bias"—is perhaps the single most important idiosyncratic determinant of goals and tactics, and hence the mode of protest.

The degree to which large scale permanent organizations of poor people are needed to promote social change remains an open question. A single event, be it a man-made riot or a natural disaster, is often enough to spark some governmental response. According to many community organizers, however, no single event can suffice to give spokesmen for an underprivileged group an authoritative voice in determining the nature of that response. These individuals stress the need to build pressure groups of poor people. For people with this organizational bias, organizational aggrandizement would always deserve a high priority. For them, showmanship alone would never be enough.

In reviewing these four sets of factors, one can dervice a fundamental hypothesis and a series of subsidiary propositions that indicate the desirability of one or another of the three modes of protest. The fundamental hypothesis relates the choice of mode of protest to the availability of resources in a given context:

> The appropriateness of a mode of protest depends upon the ability of the protest group leader to assemble resources sufficient to force concessions from a given target in a given situation. Confrontation will be favored when protest group leaders can assemble sufficient resources to create negative inducements strong enough to prompt concessions from the target. In all other cases, the protest group leader will be restricted to showmanship and organizational aggrandizement.

The subsidiary propositions consider both the level of resources necessary to engage in confrontation, and the ability of the protest group leader to mobilize them. *Confrontation* will or should be employed in those situations in which the following conditions are present:

1a. Protest group members require tangible benefits.
1b. Protest group members require quick benefits.
2a. The target has discretion to disburse benefits.
2b. The target is vulnerable to disruption—perhaps through a combination of sympathy and inexperience.
3a. There is little or no potential support from third parties. (This not only serves to eliminate the likelihood of successful showmanship but also raises the level of resources needed for achieving the necessary breakthrough in a confrontation.)
3b. The public and target regard the demands as somewhat legitimate.
3c. The public and target are at least accepting towards the use of disruptive tactics.

4a. The protest group leaders are neutral towards personal publicity.
4b. The protest group leaders are biased in favor of permanent protest organization.

Similarly, *showmanship* will or should be chosen in the following set of circumstances:

5. Protest group members will settle for symbolic victories (at least in the short run).
6a. The target has little discretion to grant benefits without some change in its rules or operating procedures.
6b. The target is powerful enough to ignore direct approaches by the protest group.
6c. The target is relatively experienced in dealing with confrontation (or has been in contact with those with such experiences) and has devised effective counter measures.
7a. There is great potential support for protest group demands among influential third parties.
7b. There is a strong prejudice against disruptive tactics on the part of target and general public.
7c. There are stiff penalties vigorously enforced against disruptive tactics.
8a. The protest group leaders seek personal publicity.
8b. The protest group leaders do not feel a need to build permanent organization.

Finally, protest as *organizational aggrandizement* will be favored to the extent that:

9a. Protest group members will settle for symbolic victories (at least in the short run).
9b. There is a need for evidence of organizational potency that is not being met by confrontation or showmanship. (Potency must be demonstrated to potential and current members, potential and current financial supporters, potential and current allies, and potential and current targets.)
10. The target is currently powerful enough to ignore direct approaches by the protest group.
11. There is great potential financial support for protest group among third parties.
12a. The protest group leaders seek personal publicity.
12b. The protest group leaders are biased in favor of permanent organization.

The theoretical framework and the hypotheses outlined in this chapter can

be validated only by a thorough review of protest activities involving a broad
spectrum of groups, targets, settings, and leadership proclivities. But both the
framework and hypotheses receive considerable support from the behavior of
the MWRO.

The theoretical framework considers the three modes of protest as tactical
alternatives facing a protest group organizer (or leader) at any given point in
time. The MWRO engaged in all three modes of protest virtually simultaneously.
The Boston model demonstrations in welfare service offices represented protest
as confrontation and relied heavily on harassment and disruption. A MWRO
"shop-in" demonstration at the Boston Army base in which the organization
called for a transfer of funds from the Defense Department towards feeding the
poor provides a good example of protest as showmanship. As previously indicated, the Boston Common "birthday of the movement demonstration" was
organized primarily to demonstrate the MWRO's ability to mobilize thousands
of members and sympathizers and hence represented protest as organizational
aggrandizement. In the latter example, the MWRO was seeking to impress a
wide variety of individuals: the target institution, financial contributors,
supporters, members and staff, as well as potential targets, contributors, supporters, members and staff.

Some welfare rights activities in Massachusetts represented hybrids of
several modes. A radio station sit-in protesting the broadcasting of the song
"Welfare Cadillac" involved confrontation but was also directed at organizational aggrandizement through a demonstration of organizational potency. The
MWRO march through the Boston streets with a hood of an automobile carried
at the head of the procession just prior to the radio station sit-in combined
showmanship and aggrandizement.

Two experiences of the MWRO are particularly useful in illustrating the
richness and the complexity of the various forms of protest as organizational
aggrandizement. The disruption of a Harvard University speaking engagement
of Secretary of Health, Education and Welfare Robert Finch was designed in
large measure to increase the experience, confidence, and visibility of a faction
of the MWRO leadership and thus lead to the strengthening of the organization.
A "shop-in" at the Cambridge branch of Sears was carried out primarily to
boost the morale of the MWRO leadership (as well as certain staff members) in
the face of disappointment. The shop-in began just minutes after a three-hour
effort to confront the state welfare commissioner had been blocked by helmeted
policemen and then totally deflated when it was revealed that the commissioner
was no longer in the building. Before anyone had any chance to fully appreciate
the extent of the failure, everyone was urged to return to the rented buses to
travel to the Cambridge department store.

The organizational mainenance needs of the MWRO have had a major
impact upon the choice of mode of protest employed. The crucial insight of
the welfare rights movement was that large numbers of welfare recipients could

be motivated to participate in organizational activities if, and only if, they were
to receive tangible benefits and if they could receive them quickly. This in turn
forced a great reliance upon confrontation, the only tactic that could provide
the required payoff in the required time span. Whatever else the MWRO organizers might have wished to attempt in the way of showmanship or aggrandizement, periodic special needs grants campaigns were necessary if membership
interest was to be maintained.

Because the potency of disruptive demonstrations was (seen as) directly
related to the numbers of individuals participating, the MWRO organizers
felt the need to expend great amounts of time and resources on insuring the
large turnout. This built-in demand for a high level of resources created a need
for organizational aggrandizement activities when successful confrontation
was not possible simply to maintain the interest of staff, contributors and
potential staff and contributors. Had the MWRO chosen to rely to a greater
extent upon showmanship, its needs in terms of staff or contributors would
have been minimized and there would, therefore, have been less pressure to
engage in organizational aggrandizement activities as well.

Both the insights and the skills of the MWRO organizers concerning the
motivation of welfare recipients would have been useless without the presence
of a target that could provide the needed tangible benefits. (As will be suggested in Chapter 9, the difficulty in discovering a similarly vulnerable target
is probably the greatest single barrier to the replication of the Boston model
for groups other than welfare recipients.)

The Massachusetts Department of Public Welfare provided an ideal target
for such a group that needed tangible benefits. Discretion to disburse supplementary benefits was located at the lowest levels of the public welfare system—
where the clientele had contact—and could be implemented by caseworkers
or their direct supervisors, many of whom were sympathetic to the needs of
recipients. This meant that successful intimidation of caseworkers could provide hundreds of dollars of benefits for welfare recipients at no cost to the
welfare rights movement.

The existence of special needs benefits provisions in the regulations also
contributed to the legitimacy of the protesters' demands. Once the Massachusetts Welfare Department had agreed to the promulgation of guidelines—
precise statements that listed all of the special needs items to which an individual was entitled and the maximum amount of money that could be spent
on each—protest groups could present detailed and specific demands with an
air of legality. This put the target on the defensive and served to encourage
potential-demonstrators. This point is also stressed in Lipsky's discussion of
the rent strike movement:

> New York City tenants enjoy the most liberal landlord–tenant laws
> in the country. Availability of the rent strike provisions allowed tenants

to violate accepted norms of landlord tenant relations while remaining within the law. . . . People were willing to participate because they were engaged in legally responsible actions.[7]

A number of additional characteristics of the welfare system in Massachusetts made it a particularly vulnerable target. Probably the most important of these was the administrative uncertainty that followed a reorganization of the state welfare system that took place just as Bill Pastreich began his organizing activities in Boston. These uncertainties contributed to the slowness with which the welfare system appeared to learn from its own mistakes and to devise effective counter measures against confrontation tactics. For month after month, what Alinsky has referred to as "the incredibly stupid blunders of the status quo" were repeated as each new local welfare rights organization confronted its target in a local welfare service office for the first time. This enabled the MWRO protest groups to benefit from the elements of surprise and target unpreparedness—the "first time factor"—for much of the existence of the organization.

The eventual disappearance of the "first time factor" made it more difficult for the MWRO to repeat its initial successes in local welfare offices confrontations. A number of the most successful demonstrations in the later phases of organizational development were directed against other targets that had less experience in dealing with confrontation. The MWRO sit-in in a Boston radio station and the disruption of Secretary Finch's speech on the Harvard campus illustrate the advantages of attacking an inexperienced or unprepared target.

The entire executive branch of the Massachusetts government was also more vulnerable than usual to confrontation tactics by militant blacks during the early MWRO organizing drives. The fear of urban riots at a time when the governor of the state was reportedly seeking higher office was a contributing factor to the first major victory—the Massachusetts Welfare Department's promulgation of furniture guidelines—won by the MWRO through the use of confrontation tactics.

Such elements of the political setting in Massachusetts as a relatively lenient trespass statute also favored the choice of confrontation tactics by the MWRO. The maximum fine for trespass during the early history of the welfare rights movement in Massachusetts was $20. Beyond this, few judges in that state were willing to impose any monetary penalty on welfare recipients convicted of unlawful trespass. The MWRO could therefore engage in protest with little to lose. A stiffening of that statute was followed by a general reduction of welfare rights militance.

Perhaps the most critical factor in the political setting of the welfare rights movement was the antipathy of the general public towards both the welfare rights goals and tactics. Most members of the public assumed a causal connection between the rising welfare rights militance and the rapidly increasing welfare budgets, and most MWRO staff members assumed that well-publicized demonstrations would, if anything, result in greater pressures to cut welfare than to liberalize the system.

Public resentment against welfare recipients played a major role in the 1970 Massachusetts gubernatorial campaign in which the incumbent made a major issue of his "reform" in which the welfare rights tactical staple of special needs grants was eliminated. In one of his widely broadcast radio advertisements, the incumbent said:

> The way it used to be, to get a new refrigerator you'd demand
> one, you'd demonstrate for one. . . . Working people have special
> needs too. But they don't get special needs payments. . . . This
> isn't money from heaven, this is taxpayers' money. And I've got a
> responsibility to see that it is . . . not wasted.[8]

A fuller discussion of welfare reform in Massachusetts is presented in Chapter 9.

This attitude on the part of the general public undoubtedly lessened the effectiveness of MWRO confrontation tactics by making it more difficult for welfare administrators to take action that might be interpreted as giving in to the unjust demands of disruptive demonstrators. But it also ruled out reliance upon showmanship as a major tactical staple. Wherever possible, MWRO efforts to activate sympathetic third parties were carried out only through specialized means of communications such as the newsletters and periodicals of voluntary associations such as the Eastern Massachusetts Chapter of the National Association of Social Workers and the Massachusetts Social Welfare Workers Movement (SWWM). In addition the MWRO organizers played a key role in the founding of the Massachusetts Citizens Committee to Change Welfare whose newsletter functioned as a prime conduit of information about welfare rights activities to sympathetic members of the general public. Finally, the MWRO staff periodically sent a specially prepared packet of newspaper clippings and other organizational information to about two dozen key allies and financial supporters through "first family mailings."

The possibility of negative reaction by third parties to protest demonstrations, and hence the presence of major constraints against reliance upon showmanship, is by no means confined to the welfare rights movement. In fact, almost all militant and disruptive tactics can be counted upon to win the disapproval of large numbers of Americans.[9]

The personal characteristics of the MWRO organizers also contributed to their primary reliance upon confrontation rather than showmanship. MWRO staff were always scrupulously careful to avoid personal publicity in connection with demonstrations. In the case of the MWRO—as in the Alinsky-run organizing efforts—the need to build and maintain a permanent organizational structure was taken as an article of faith. Given this organizational bias and the constraints upon mobilizing large numbers of welfare recipients, it was inevitable that the welfare rights movement would have had to rely on confrontations in the welfare office if it were to exist as its organizers would want.

The MWRO organizational bias can be contrasted with Lipsky's description of the New York City rent strikers and their leader Jesse Gray. Gray's inattention to organizational procedures in effect ruled out any possibility of mobilizing enough followers in order to put economic pressure on individual landlords. For the most part, this ruled out confrontation as a tactic and dictated a strategy based upon the mass media and upon reference publics, and showmanship because the most appropriate mode of protest.

In sum, the MWRO was impelled towards a basic reliance upon confrontation by a convergence of factors relating to organizational maintenance needs, the nature of the target, the political setting, and the personal characteristics of its staff. At the same time, however, there were a number of specific circumstances that prompted occasional use of showmanship and organizational aggrandizement. The showmanship at the Boston army base was predicated in large part upon the desirability of linking welfare rights activities with the broad range of anti-war demonstrations connected with the Vietnam moratorium, and drawing closer to other militant groups as potential allies. The aggrandizement of the Boston Common rally reflects a need to prove organizational potency, a requirement that is probably common to all pressure groups.

The four factors discussed in this chapter indicate both the general organizational style of protest as well as the times when a group departs from its usual style to engage in other modes. In closing however, it should be stressed that both the choice of a primary mode of protest and the decisions regarding departure from this mode are not made as rationally as is suggested in this chapter. In the case of the MWRO—and in all likelihood other protest organizations—decisions concerning the appropriate mode of protest were made incrementally in a complex process involving both calculation and intuition. The theoretical framework herein described is therefore an effort to abstract from that process those elements with which a protest group leader would agree if he were in possession of all relevant facts and were totally rational.

9 Accomplishments of the Welfare Rights Movement

Although the Massachusetts Welfare Rights Organization exhibited notable strength at the grassroots level by organizing thousands of welfare recipients, it did not meet with comparable success with respect to its policy-oriented goals with the state government. Similarly, despite some successes, the National Welfare Rights Organization has not won any of its major objectives with the Congress of the United States or the Department of Health, Education and Welfare. The welfare rights movement did, however, lay the foundation for greater influence in the future through its recognition as a legitimate participant in the policy-making process, its acquisition of allies in other, more powerful organizations, and through its impact upon the lives of its membership, leaders, organizing staff, and upon other students of community organization.

The rapidly rising welfare rolls—and hence welfare budgets—in the late 1960s combined with widespread public concerns with "welfare chiseling" led politicians in Massachusetts and the other major industrial states to view public welfare expenditures as the prime candidates for budget cut. These increases in welfare rolls were not, in general, due to welfare rights activities. As indicated in Chapter 3, the Boston model devoted its attention to those who were already welfare recipients. This pattern was, for the most-part, repeated throughout the country, and a recent study of the growth of the welfare caseload in this period concluded that the "NWRO's contribution to the rising welfare rolls has been largely indirect, the unintended effect of other activities."[1]

As a result of this trend in welfare politics, the MWRO and welfare rights affiliates in other states were placed on the defensive for most of their existence. The bulk of their lobbying efforts were attempts to defeat or modify legislation and administrative action that they opposed rather than efforts to promote improvements in the welfare system.

Because special needs grants were so crucial to Boston model and other welfare rights organizing efforts, actions by state governments to abolish these grants and institute "flat grant" systems were more of a blow to the welfare rights movement than the more publicized efforts to cut basic welfare payments. The two states in which the welfare rights movement achieved its greatest grassroots successes, New York and Massachusetts, were the first to institute flat grants. The welfare rights affiliates in those states were virtually powerless to prevent the adoption of flat grant, and other states have since begun to follow suit. Although welfare administrators denied that the flat grant was instituted to "get" welfare rights, it is clear the principal policy change that followed

141

welfare rights organizing activities was the institution of—or at least the hastening of—the worst possible change in public assistance laws from the point of view of movement organizers. In New York, for example, administrators stressed such benefits of a flat grant system as the elimination of the demeaning need for a recipient to request supplementary grants from his caseworker as well as the gains in equity when all families of a given size received the same amount of money. Similar arguments were used in New Jersey. In both cases, however, official concern with the demeaning aspects and lack of equity in special needs did not appear to develop until after welfare rights groups had become active.

The relationship between the institution of the flat grant and welfare rights organizing was treated fairly candidly in Massachusetts. The MWRO activities received considerable coverage in the newspapers and on radio and television. Many people in Massachusetts apparently associated welfare rights demonstrations with rising welfare costs and assumed the former caused the latter, all of which served to make welfare an increasingly controversial public issue. A number of state legislators gained publicity by investigating alleged welfare fraud and by introducing bills to cut welfare costs. The governor made his ability to resist welfare demonstrators and his institution of the flat grant a major issue in his re-election campaign in 1970. Three of his radio advertisements mentioned welfare demonstrators and one of them was entirely devoted to an explanation of flat grant. The message the governor sought to convey to his public was the following:

> The way it used to be, to get a new refrigerator, you'd demand one, you'd demonstrate for one. We've stopped something called special needs payments. There were hundreds of these . . . lots of loopholes and frankly, lots of temptations. Working people have special needs too but they don't get special needs payments. . . . Governor Sargent has cut down the cost of welfare—and the chance of fraud . . .
>
> We've been demonstrated against and we've been threatened. But we haven't been afraid to say "no." Sargent said "no" to extra pay raises, "no" to extra welfare payments . . . Sargent turned the welfare system around. The flat grant payments, they're now in effect.[2]

In retrospect, the special needs grant system appears to have survived prior to welfare rights activity primarily because of the pervasive ignorance of its existence. This permitted it to remain a marginal appendage to the basic system of disbursing welfare payments. Once the welfare rights movement organizing activity contributed to its visibility—to recipients and the public—and to its costs, the special needs grant system became a liability. Since information about furniture, clothing, and other benefits had also been disseminated by poverty lawyers, community action agency personnel, social workers, and others, there is little reason to doubt that special needs grants were doomed anyhow, and that regardless of future activities of welfare rights organizers, the adoption of the flat grant system will continue in other states.

The MWRO leaders and staff as well as welfare rights activists in other states perceived the flat grant as a major threat to the continued functioning of the movement, although many local affiliates were already in a period of decline by the time of the implementation of the flat grant. But in Massachusetts, as elsewhere, the efforts to fight the flat grant were sporadic and ineffectual. Despite sympathetic coverage from many New York newspapers and television stations— "here is a blind man who will no longer have special needs money to buy dog food for his seeing eye dog"—the flat grant never became a major public issue in that state. The New York Citywide Coordinating Committee of Welfare (Rights) Groups demonstrated against the flat grant and other welfare cuts at local welfare offices and the state capital, but the absence of any possibility of an immediately realizable pay-off for these activities led to a downplaying of these tactics.

As already indicated, few MWRO organizers or lay leaders saw any possibility of dissuading the governor from his announced intention to end special needs. The MWRO demonstrations against the flat grant were thus planned largely for internal consumption rather than to influence the political system.

Although unable to persuade the governor, the MWRO did have some success in convincing other social welfare voluntary associations to join it in the fight against the flat grant. Most MWRO lobbying efforts against the flat grant and proposed welfare cutbacks were taken in conjunction with allies in the Massachusetts Welfare Coalition. The Welfare Coalition included welfare rights leaders along with representatives of the Eastern Massachusetts chapter of the National Association of Social Workers, the Massachusetts Council of Churches, the Catholic Charities of Greater Boston, the Family Service Association of Greater Boston, the United Community Services of Greater Boston, and the Social Workers Guild. Since there were a number of reasonable arguments—such as the greater equity involved[a]—in favor of the flat grant, it is

---

[a]Other arguments in favor of the flat grant included the reduction of caseworkers discretion in the disbursement of benefits and the fact that so few recipients had been aware of special needs regulations that this disbursement had not been equitable. Since most flat grant proposals have taken the funds previously allocated for supplementary welfare payments and redistributed them equally among all recipients, supporters of the flat grant have argued that its implementation has meant an increase in benefits for most recipients. Some social welfare leaders have endorsed the concept of a flat grant, but only when the basic benefit level is high enough to support a minimum adequate standard of living. Until that time, they supported special needs grants as a "cushion" to cover emergencies. Welfare rights organizers have endorsed the cushion concept as well, but regardless of the basic benefit level, organizers would have favored retention of the special needs grants to provide organizing tools.

likely that the Massachusetts Conference on Social Welfare might have been more receptive to the governor's proposal were it not for the staunch opposition to it from a recipients' group.

In recent years, the leaders of the Massachusetts Welfare Coalition have continued to meet regularly with each other and have been consulted by legislative officials and gubernatorial aides. Although these leaders were unable to prevent the implementation of the flat grant at the time, the Coalition did succeed in softening or eliminating most of the harshest provisions in public assistance legislation and in winning liberal interpretations of that legislation by Welfare Department administrators.

While none of the religious, charitable, or social welfare allies of the MWRO in the Welfare Coalition were notably influential in state politics, the MWRO affiliation with the Coalition did have a number of positive effects in furthering welfare rights goals. Association with the well-respected groups in the Coalition gave the MWRO representatives a measure of increased respectability and—at least in coordination with other Coalition members—increased access to policymakers. Secondly, by winning the support of these more reputable organizations, the MWRO also presumably increased the public acceptability of its own positions.

The results of the MWRO efforts to "fight the flat grant" were in many ways typical of the general pattern of welfare rights lobbying. The most positive of these results on both the state and national level were increased recognition as a legitimate participant in the policy-making process by representing a major constituency as well as a significant impact upon the public positions of other voluntary associations. Neither of these could be directly translated into political influence, but both were steps in the direction of future acquisition of power.

Welfare rights leaders and organizers won the right to be consulted from both state and federal officials. When the organization was in its strongest period, MWRO lay leaders met regularly with the Massachusetts Welfare Commissioner and his staff; they were asked for comments in the process of choosing a replacement when the incumbent commissioner resigned. The Welfare Department routinely sent copies of its "State Letters" and other administrative directives to the MWRO statewide office within months of the organization's founding.

On the national level, officials of the Department of Health, Education and Welfare have also met regularly with NWRO leaders and staff. NWRO leaders were consulted by the White House staff during the drafting of the Family Assistance Plan. One HEW official has indicated that this access has led to subtle changes in himself and his colleagues when they prepare legislative proposals or administrative regulations:

> In the past, we used to consider what the reaction of Congress
> might be, how the states would respond. We used to consider the

social work establishment as well. Now we've begun to consider the recipients too: what would they think about what we're doing.[3]

Through the efforts of welfare rights leaders and staff and their allies in the legal profession, the Department of Health, Education and Welfare has been forced into taking a firmer stand against the states whose welfare laws and practices have been out of compliance with federal regulations. While NWRO lobbying efforts have included the filing of lawsuits, most efforts have been centered upon negotiations calling for out-of-court settlements. As a result of these efforts, a number of changes in HEW regulations have been made, hearings to determine state compliance with federal regulations have been held, and in some cases, machinery to cut off state welfare funds for non-compliance has been set in motion. It is difficult to assess the extent to which these changes would have resulted through the actions of poverty lawyers alone without any backing from a mass-based recipients organization, but in any event, these victories have represented victories for the NWRO.

Perhaps the ultimate measure of federal government acceptance of the NWRO was its willingness to disburse monies to the organization. Although the move drew vigorous opposition by elements within the government and within the movement, in late 1968, the Department of Labor awarded the NWRO a grant of over $400,000 to help monitor the Work Incentive (WIN) Program and to increase recipient knowledge of its provisions. Several welfare rights affiliates bitterly opposed accepting the grant on the grounds that it might compromise the independence of the movement, but their fears appear to have been without basis. The receipt of federal funds did not prevent continued demonstrations in the Washington, D.C., welfare offices or even a sit-in in the office of the Secretary of Health, Education and Welfare.

It is ironical that this increased recognition of the welfare rights movement has coincided with the deterioration of many of its oldest and most powerful local affiliates. In part, this seeming paradox can be explained by the continued organizing of new local groups to maintain the appearance of constant grass-roots activity; as older groups sink into inaction, newer ones move in to take their place and continue to gain headlines through demonstrations and other activities.

Even more importantly, the inability of the local welfare rights organizations to maintain a high level of membership participation over the years has not particularly weakened the state and national welfare rights organizations because the local groups have already served their major function of establishing the credibility of those leaders who claim to be representing a major constituency. Lobbying activity on the state and national level does not generally depend upon the mobilization of large numbers of individual and the creation of the coercive potential called for in the Boston model. Instead all that is needed is a small number of articulate spokesmen who can convincingly claim to represent large numbers of individuals. In the years since the first nationwide welfare rights rallies in June of 1966, the NWRO has developed a number of colorful and forceful leaders who have since become familiar figures in government offices and the meetings of social welfare and church-related voluntary associations. Their claim to legitimacy has been based on their representing a movement with tens of thousands of members, as evidenced by well-publicized rallies. As long as a handful of demonstrations continue to occur to remind people of what has happened in the past, the spokesmen can maintain the impression that their constituency persists.

Although welfare rights activity has slowed down in many areas, the growing reputation of the movement has brought it somewhat better—though far from thorough—coverage for many of its activities in features and documentaries as well as hard news stories.[4] This in turn further helped maintain the reputation and credibility of the leaders and national staff of the movement.

In part, because of this growing legitimacy, the welfare rights movement became an increasingly powerful goad to many leading liberal and radical organizations. Groups that had traditionally claimed to be representing the poor found it embarrassing to be endorsing positions that were then rejected by the elected representatives of the intended beneficiaries of their good works. Social work organizations have proven especially vulnerable to the welfare rights exploitation of sympathy and guilt. (The role of the MWRO in convincing the members of the Massachusetts Welfare Coalition to oppose the flat grant has already been discussed.) The National Conference on Social Welfare has for several years made a practice of inviting NWRO members to their meetings only to have themselves harangued by their guests and sometimes submitted to semi-coercive "shake-downs"—blocking the exits wuntil cash donations have been made.[5]

The welfare rights movement has also found some elements within the Democratic party to be moderately responsive to its appeals. A small delegation from the MWRO to the state Democratic convention in 1970 won the inclusion of the following clause in the party platform:

> We accept our own responsibility in the Commonwealth to provide the kind of welfare system which meets our standards of humanitarianism, justice, and feasibility. To that end we support the following:
> ... A system of income maintenance based on the Bureau of Labor Statistics standards adjusted to regional cost of living standards and future changes in that cost ...
> ... Retention of the "special needs" category as the only humane system that provides any cushion against emergencies as long as welfare grants remain at any inadequate level.[6]

In essence the Democratic platform supported the welfare rights goal of "$5500

or fight," since that was the level based on Bureau of Labor Statistics calcula-
tions, and opposed the flat grant. Neither of these platform planks had much
impact upon political events in the state, but they were symbolic of the growing
acceptance of the positions espoused by the MWRO.

Although the extent of its influence has been widely disputed, it is clear
that the National Welfare Rights Organization did play a role in the defeat of
President Nixon's welfare reform legislation. A NWRO presentation to the
Democratic Policy Council was followed by that body's adoption of a resolution expressing support for raising the income floor in President Nixon's proposed Family Assistance Plan by several thousand dollars. Senator Eugene
McCarthy was persuaded to introduce the NWRO-drafted Adequate Income
Act of 1970, and approximately 30 members of the House of Representatives,
including the entire Black Caucus, introduced legislation calling for a guaranteed annual income at the level endorsed by the NWRO—currently $6500 for
a family of four.

Welfare rights staff members have claimed that they were a major factor
in convincing three liberal Democrats on the Senate Finance Committee to
vote against the Family Assistance Plan in 1970. These claims received some
substantiation from independent sources who also attribute to the NWRO a
degree of influence in shaping the direction of Congressional debate on welfare
reform.

The impact of the welfare rights movement upon Republican policy-makers
has been considerably less pronounced. Welfare rights leaders were consulted by
White House staff members in the formulation of the Family Assistance Plan,
but there has thus far been little evidence that the NWRO suggestions at these
consultations had any significant impact in the shaping of the legislative proposals.[7]

Not only has the welfare rights movement served as a prod to liberal organizations and politicians, but it has also met with success in influencing more
radical groups as well. Welfare rights members were the major exception to the
failure of the antiwar movement to attract the poor and minority groups to
their rallies. Welfare rights leaders spoke at antiwar rallies in Washington, Boston,
and elsewhere, and in response to this, a number of radical groups broadened
their goals to include both foreign and domestic policy. The People's Coalition
for Peace and Justice, sponsor of many of the May 1971 antiwar rallies in Washington, D.C., included both withdrawal from Indochina and a guaranteed annual
income of $6500 for a family of four among its demands;[8] its demonstrators
visited the Department of Health, Education and Welfare as well as the Selective
Service System.

It should be recognized that—with the possible exception of the radical
groups—the achievements of the welfare rights movement in winning support
or endorsements were not due to the power of the movement in terms of its
ability to mobilize large numbers of recipients for demonstrations. Instead the

impact was derived from the welfare rights standing as a recognized spokesman for a significant interest group, and a highly refined ability to play upon middle-class guilt. Thus, for example, the NWRO approach to the Democratic Policy Council did not make any allusions to the voting power of its membership. It simply advanced the position that, "if the Democratic party wants to represent poor people whose interests it has traditionally championed," it would have to adopt the welfare rights proposals including opening the Democratic Policy Council membership to "representatives of organized poor people."[9]

In short, the failings of the Boston model and other attempts at local group maintenance were not fatal to the National Welfare Rights Organizations attempts to influence policy on the national and state levels because these attempts, unlike the local welfare office confrontations, did not require the continued ability to mobilize large numbers of welfare recipients. Unless it proves able to mobilize at least a token fraction of their constituency from time to time, however, it does not appear likely that the NWRO spokesmen can maintain their legitimacy indefinitely.

Despite the sharp decline in grassroots welfare rights activity in recent years, the movement will continue to have an impact upon the political system through continued lobbying as well as the changes it has brought about in the lives of its participants and in their future political activity. The impact of the welfare rights movement upon the lives of the general membership is difficult to isolate. Impressionistic evidence from both the MWRO case study and the single published monograph on the subject[10] suggests that most AFDC recipients do not belong to voluntary associations. The fact that tens of thousands of recipients did join welfare rights organizations and did win considerable cash benefits indicates some changes in their lives but more importantly suggests the possibility of altered attitudes as a result of these experiences. Both the MWRO experience and monograph suggest that welfare rights activity may have reduced feelings of powerlessness.[11]

For a small number of recipients, the welfare rights movement has provided a channel for personal upward mobility. A few lay leaders who entered into the public forum through welfare rights have parlayed these positions into broader community roles in other organizations and in governmental bodies. Former leaders of the now defunct Mothers for Adequate Welfare moved into positions in the Boston and Massachusetts governments and held them long after their group disintegrated. MWRO lay leaders did the same thing; they gained positions on Welfare Department advisory councils, community action agency neighborhood boards, and such private groups oriented towards the problems of poverty as the Massachusetts Conference on Social Welfare and the Harvard Community Health Plan.

In holding such positions in the community, former leaders of welfare rights groups apply skills they learned in the movement. There is little doubt that they are more effective in whatever they attempt as a result of their welfare rights experiences.

Probably the greatest future impact of the welfare rights movement, however, lies with the lessons it has taught community organizers. Many of the ideas behind the Boston model were common knowledge to community organizers before the welfare rights movement got underway. The Prospectus for New York City's Mobilization for Youth (MFY) antipoverty program suggested the usefulness of "indigenous disadvantaged" to help organize the community, the need to organize along ethnic and racial lines, and the choice of issues that were at once highly visible and gave promise of immediate pay-off.[12] It remained for the welfare rights movement to demonstrate how these insights could in fact be put into action on a nationwide basis—and to demonstrate the pitfalls involved in doing so.

As suggested in Chapter 5, the MWRO—and to a lesser extent other welfare rights affiliates throughout the country—served as "schools for organizing." The welfare rights movement provided on-the-job training for hundreds of would-be activists; more than a hundred were involved in Massachusetts alone during a two-year period. Some former MWRO staff members returned to school and are engaged in efforts to integrate their experiences with the academic literature on community organizing. Others have remained active within the welfare rights movement and in organizing other groups around other issues.

The final assessment of the impact of the welfare rights movement, therefore, cannot be made until the experience of the Boston model manifests itself in the form of accomplishments on the part of the welfare rights "alumni." Participation in the MWRO provided the opportunity to transform the potentialities inherent in organizing people around tangible benefits into realities. Whether in universities or in the streets, graduates of the MWRO school for organizing are seeking to discover other organizing tools—comparable to the Welfare Department's special needs grants—in the hope of applying the logic of the Boston model—with appropriate modifications to minimize its weaknesses in group maintenance—to other contexts.

APPENDIXES

Appendix A
Sites of MWRO Affiliates

Adams

Beverly

Boston (20 groups)

Bourne

Brockton

Brookline

Cambridge (2 groups)

Chelsea

Falmouth

Framingham

Haverhill

Holyoke

Hyannis

Lawrence

Lowell

Lynn

Malden

Martha's Vineyard

New Bedford (2 groups)

Newton

North Adams

Onset

Pittsfield

Plymouth

Salem

Somerville (2 groups)

Springfield (6 groups)

Waltham

Watertown

Worcester

Appendix B
MWRO Forms

_____ **WELFARE OFFICE**   **LOCAL GROUP**

DATE _____   **MASS. WELFARE**

DEAR _____   **RIGHTS ORGANIZATION**
           welfare worker

FURNITURE REQUEST FORM

The following are the furniture items that I am lacking in my home and need in order to be brought up to minimum standards. I expect an answer to my request within two weeks.

KITCHEN

_____ table and four chairs	1 set per house		70.00
_____ extra chairs	1 for each person over 4		15.00 ea.
_____ high chair or low chair	as needed	durable quality	20.00
_____ refrigerator	family of 5 or less	11 to 12 cubic ft.	150.00
_____ refrigerator	family of 6 or more	14 cubic ft.	200.00
_____ washing machine	family of 2 or more	12 lb. capacity	155.00 + installation
_____ range (gas on gas)		gas where available	150.00 + installation
_____ parlor heater	no central heating		(cost at local gas co.)
_____ dish cabinet	as needed		35.00
_____ utility cabinet	as needed		35.00

BEDROOM

_____ bed (full or twin)	as needed	metal frame $14.00 head board 18.00 inner spring 35.00 mattress 35.00	102.00
_____ bunk bed	as needed	hardwood frame	125.00
_____ dresser or chest	1 per 2 persons	hardwood frame-4 draw	60.00
_____ mirror	as needed		20.00
_____ crib	as needed	hardwood panels	30.00
_____ crib mattress	as needed		10.00
_____ playpen and pad	as needed	hardwood or nylon mesh	20.00
_____ stroller or convertible	as needed	steel frame, vinyl cover	30.00
_____ pillows	1 person		3.00

LIVING ROOM

_____ sofa	1 per home	durable quality	130.00
_____ sofa bed			140.00
_____ chairs	2 per home	hardwood frame	40.00 each
_____ lamps, table or floor	1 per room		12.50 each

OTHER REQUESTS:

1. Telephone _____   SIGNATURE _____

2. _____   NAME (Print) _____

3. _____   ADDRESS (Print)_____

4. _____   _____

*NOTE: YOU MAY SPEND UP TO 10% MORE THAN THESE PRICES

Massachusetts Welfare Rights Organization, 17 Brookline Street, Cambridge, Mass., 864-2980

Welfare Office _____

Date: _____

Dear: _____

Welfare worker

Local Group of Massachusetts
Welfare Rights Organization

CLOTHING REQUEST FORM

Age Group	Under 7 yrs	7–12	13–20
GIRLS:			
2 dresses	$ 5 each _____	$ 6 each _____	$ 9 each _____
1 pr. shoes	6.50 _____	7.50 _____	8.00 _____
1 sweater	4.00 _____	5.00 _____	7.00 _____
1 winter coat	15.00 _____	21.00 _____	24.00 _____
1 pr. boots	5.00 _____	6.00 _____	7.00 _____
1 sweater	4.00 _____	6.00 _____	8.00 _____
BOYS			
2 shirts	2.50 @ _____	3.00 @ _____	3.50 @ _____
2 slacks	4.00 @ _____	7.00 @ _____	9.00 @ _____
1 pr. shoes	7.00 _____	9.00 _____	11.00 _____
1 sweater	4.00 _____	5.00 _____	7.00 _____
1 winter coat	15.00 _____	17.50 _____	22.00 _____
1 sweater	4.00 _____	6.00 _____	7.00 _____

ADULT: 1 winter coat $50.00 _____

INFANT (0–6 months) Layette $50.00 _____

I base my request for these items on State letters 240A and 240C which provide for special clothing allowances for the above items under points 2, 3, and 4 of State Letter 240A.

2. Clothing essential to school attendance of child
3. Replacement of clothing for a child due to unusual growth or size
4. Clothing essential for pre-school children or for younger children attending school for the first time.

I therefore under points 2 ____ , 3, ____ and 4 ____ request the above items of clothing and the money to purchase them.

SIGNATURE: _____

Name (Print) _____

Address _____

TO: SUBDIVISION OF APPEALS
DEPARTMENT OF PUBLIC WELFARE
Location: _____

DATE: _____

I wish to appeal the decision of the Welfare Office at _____

_____ , Massachusetts, with regard to:

1.   Grant Inadequate

2.   _____ request of _____ denied or not acted upon

3.

4.

5.

I request a FAIR HEARING BEFORE A REFEREE and that a stenographic record be
made of the hearing.

I request that all future correspondence and negotiation in connection with this matter be
to and with my attorney, of 17 Brookline Street, Cambridge, Massachusetts. Also send
copies of all future correspondence to me and to my local WRO group.

I also request that a copy of the social worker's summary be sent to my said attorney and
that my said attorney have the opportunity to review my case record sufficiently prior to
the scheduled hearing date to enable him to properly prepare my case.

I also request transportation, babysitting, and other necessary expenses related to my
preparing for and appearing at the fair hearing.

NAME _____
          Print   first name   last name

ADDRESS _____
                        number   street

CITY OR TOWN _____ , Massachusetts

Please inform my lawyer and the chairman of my group _____ of
the date of my hearing.

SIGNATURE_____

Notes

Notes

Chapter 1
Introduction

1. Edward C. Banfield, *The Unheavenly City* (Boston: Little, Brown, 1970), p.130.
2. In Ralph Kramer's *Participation of the Poor* (Englewood Cliffs, New Jersey: Prentice-Hall, 1969), the author discusses "two opposing orientations toward the cause of poverty . . . both of which were sanctioned by OEO," (p. 3). One of them held that poverty persisted because of the powerlessness of the poor and that "only as low-income persons were organized and mobilized as an effective pressure group could they begin to influence city hall, the schools, and the welfare and housing bureaucracies" (p. 13). Daniel P. Moynihan lists four major interpretations of the term community action in his *Maximum Feasible Misunderstanding* (New York: Free Press, 1969), one of which was "confronting the power structure, as in the Industrial Areas Foundation of Saul Alinsky" (p. 168).
3. The figure of 75,000 has been claimed by the NWRO on many occasions. See for example, "Welfare Rights as Organizational Weapon: An Interview with George Wiley," *Social Policy*, July/August 1970, pp. 61–62, and a full page advertisement taken out by "Friends of NWRO" in *The New York Times*, Sunday, December 21, 1969, Section IV, p. 9. "Welfare—The Shame of a Nation," an article in *Newsweek*, February 8, 1971 credited the NWRO with 125,000 members.
4. For a discussion of the leading arguments pertaining to the culture of poverty, see Charles A. Valentine, *Culture and Poverty: Critique and Counterproposals* (Chicago: University of Chicago Press, 1968).

Chapter 2
The Historical Content

1. Gilbert Steiner, *Social Insecurity* (Chicago: Rand-McNally, 1966), pp. 153, 154, 157.
2. This chapter has been compiled primarily from notes of personal conversations with welfare rights staff on the national and statewide level and whatever documents have been available. The best single source available concerning the history of the NWRO is the unpublished doctoral dissertation of William Whitaker, "The Determinants of Social Movement Success," The Florence Heller School for Advanced Studies in Social Welfare, Brandeis University, May, 1970.

3. Richard Cloward and Frances Fox Piven, "The Weight of the Poor: A Strategy to End Poverty," *The Nation*, May 2, 1966.
4. Frances Fox Piven and Richard Cloward, *Regulating the Poor: The Functions of Public Welfare* (New York: Pantheon, 1970), p. 327n.
5. An excellent summary and analysis of the history of the MAWs can be found in Donald Stewart's unpublished paper, "Welfare and the Politics of Protest," dated May 1969. The discussion of the MAWs in this chapter is based primarily on that source and conversations with Stewart, Bill Pastreich, and former members of that organization.
6. The early history of the MWRO, is recounted in Mary Ann Fiske's unpublished Masters thesis, "The Politics of the Claiming Minority." Cornell University, September, 1971.
7. For a detailed analysis of the negotiations, see Michael Piore's unpublished paper, "Racial Negotiations: The Massachusetts Welfare Confrontations," February, 1970.
8. *NOW!* Washington: NWRO, February 14, 1969.
9. "NWRO Membership Report for 1969."

Chapter 3
The Boston Model for Grassroots Organization

1. Charles Silberman, *Crisis in Black and White* (New York: Vintage, (1964), p.334.
2. Ibid., p. 335.

Chapter 4
The Difficulties in Local Group Maintenance

1. An article in *The New York Times*, March 27, 1969, contained a statement by the management of Sears that it was company policy to "grant credit to applicants of limited income—including welfare recipients—and do so if they are able and plan their purchasing to fit their income and other obligations. This practice applies equally to all customers regardless of the source or the amount of their income."
2. James Q. Wilson, "The Strategy of Protest," *Journal of Conflict Resolution*, September, 1961, pp. 291–303.
3. Michael Lipsky, "Protest as a Political Resource," *American Political Science Review*, December, 1968, pp. 1144–1158.

Chapter 5
The MWRO Staff

1. Saul Alinsky, *The Professional Radical: Conversations with Saul Alinsky*, ed. Marion K. Sanders (New York: Harper and Row, 1970), p. 68; Perennial Library edition. Copyright © 1965, 1969, and 1970 by Marion K. Sanders and Saul Alinsky.

2. Frances Fox Piven and Richard Cloward, *Regulating the Poor* (New York: Pantheon, 1971), p. 329n.
3. Peter Matthiessen, *Sal Si Puedes* (New York: Random House, 1969), p. 57.
4. Jack Newfield, *A Prophetic Minority* (New York: Signet, 1970), p. 72.
5. Inge Powell Bell, *CORE and the Strategy of Non-violence* (New York: Random House, 1968), p. 189.
6. Alinsky, *The Professional Radical*, p. 83.
7. This quotation and all other goal-related statements in this chapter have been derived from the responses from a questionnaire administered to 45 MWRO staff members in 1970.
8. Bell, see pages 69 and 88.
9. Howard Zinn, *SNCC: The New Abolitionists* (Boston: Beacon Press, 1965), pp. 9, 10, 244.
10. Newfield, p. 85.
11. Kenneth Keniston, *Young Radicals* (New York: Harcourt, Brace, and World, 1968), pp. 14, 230.
12. Paul Jacobs and Saul Landau, *The New Radicals* (New York: Vintage, 1966), p. 58.
13. *Ibid.*, p. 67.
14. Zinn, p. 227.
15. Keniston, p. 262.
16. Bell, p.77.
17. Keniston, p. 30
18. Jacobs and Landau, p. 4.
19. Jacobs and Landau, p. 29.
20. Keniston, pp. 151-52. Emphasis is the author's.
21. Jacobs and Landau, p. 22.
22. Zinn, pp. 7, 13.
23. Keniston, p. 181.
24. Ibid., p. 36.
25. Newfield, pp. 23, 93.
26. Saul Alinsky, *Reveille for Radicals* (New York: Vintage, 1969), p. xiv.
27. Ibid., p. 22.
28. Warren Haggstrom, "The Power of the Poor," in Frank Reissman, et al, eds., *Mental Health of the Poor* (New York: Free Press, 1964), p. 221.
29. Alinsky, *The Professional Radical*, p. 33.
30. Newfield, p. 88.
31. Jacobs and Landau, p. 30.
32. Ibid., p. 154.
33. Keniston, p. 168.
34. Newfield, p. 92.
35. Keniston, p. 167.
36. Jacobs and Landau, p. 21.
37. Zinn, p. 268.
38. Keniston, p. 162.
39. Newfield, p. 103.
40. Jacobs and Landau, p. 19.

41. Newfield, p. 62.
42. Keniston, p. 154.
43. Newfield, p. 155.

Chapter 6
The MWRO Lay Leadership

1. The data in this chapter for the Massachusetts AFDC population has been
   taken from a document published by the Commonwealth of Massachusetts
   Department of Public Welfare entitled "Study of the Standard Family
   Budget (Aid to Families with Dependent Children)," dated December 3,
   1969. Information concerning MWRO leaders is derived from interviews
   with 16 key leaders.
2. U.S. Bureau of the Census data quoted in *The New York Times Encyclo-
   pedic Almanac: 1971* (New York: The New York Times, 1970), p. 518.
3. A summary of previous studies relating social class and organizational
   affiliation can be found in Nicholas Babchuck and Alan Booth, "Voluntary
   Association Membership: A Longitudinal Analysis," *American Sociological
   Review,* February, 1969, pp. 31–45.
4. Edward C. Banfield, *The Unheavenly City* (Boston: Little, Brown, 1970).
   See especially pages 45–66.
5. See for example Seymour Martin Lipset, et al, *Union Democracy* (Garden
   City, New York: Doubleday, 1962), especially Chapter 18.
6. Herbert McClosky, "Issue Conflict and Consensus among Party Leaders,"
   American Political Science Review, June, 1960.
7. Norman Luttberg and Harmon Ziegler, "Attitude Consensus and Conflict
   in an Interest Group," *American Political Science Review,* September,
   1966.
8. Saul Alinsky, *Reveille for Radicals* (New York: Vintage, 1969), p. 59.

Chapter 7
Welfare Rights and the Study of
Voluntary Associations

1. Peter B. Clark and James Q. Wilson, "Incentive Systems: A Theory of
   Organizations," *Administrative Science Quarterly* (September, 1961),
   pp. 137, 130.
2. Ibid., pp. 134–35.
3. Ibid., p. 138.
4. Philip Selznick, "Internal Tendencies in Bureaucracy" in William Glaser
   and David Sills, (eds.), *The Government of Associations* (Totawa, New
   Jersey: Bedminster Press, 1966), p. 190.
5. Clark and Wilson, p. 140.
6. Information concerning the Consumers Education and Protection Association (CEPA) was compiled from "Moneysworth: The Consumer Newsletter," Vol. 1, No. 3, November 16,1970, pp. 1–2, and materials provided
   by CEPA, International, 6048 Ogontz Avenue, Philadelphia, Pennsylvania.

7. Clark and Wilson, p. 140.
8. Ibid., p. 151.
9. Samuel Eldersveld, *Political Parties: A Behavioral Analysis* (Chicago: Rand McNally, 1964). See especially chapters 9 and 11.
10. Norman Luttberg and Harmon Ziegler, "Attitude Consensus and Conflict in an Interest Group," *American Political Science Review,* September, 1966.
11. Graham Allison, "Conceptual Models of the Cuban Missile Crisis," *American Political Science Review* (September, 1969).
12. Gilbert Steiner, *The State of Welfare* (Washington: Brookings, 1971), p. 288.
13. Donald Stewart, "Welfare and the Politics of Protest," unpublished paper dated May, 1969.
14. Steiner, p. 285.
15. Lee Rainwater, "Neighborhood Action and Lower-Class Life-Style" in John B. Turner (ed.) *Neighborhood Organization for Community Action* (New York: National Association of Social Workers, 1968), p. 31.
16. Robert Dahl, *A Preface to Democratic Theory* (Chicago: University of Chicago, 1956), p. 145.
17. Nicholas Babchuck and Alan Booth, "Voluntary Association Membership: A Longitudinal Analysis," *American Sociological Review,* February, 1969.
18. Rainwater, p. 31.
19. See for example the statistics quoted in Marvin Olsen, "Social and Political Participation of Blacks," *American Sociological Review*, August, 1970. Michael Lipsky, in his *Protest in City Politics* (Chicago: Rand McNally, 1970), has concluded that

Perhaps more common than protest groups which obtain public recognition are those instances where relatively powerless groups wishing to effect public policy, are unable to gain attention for the very reasons they are considered powerless. They lack the minimum resources necessary to initiate or sustain protest activities which would bring their demands before a wider public. . . . They are free to organize. In organization there may be strength. But it is strength severely diluted by the structure of group political life in American cities. (pp. 202–3)

20. Rainwater, p. 30.
21. Ibid., p. 32.
22. Ibid., p. 33.
23. Mancur Olson, *The Logic of Collective Action* (Cambridge, Harvard University, 1965), p. 2.
24. Abraham Maslow, *Motivation and Personality* (2nd ed.) (New York: Harper and Row, 1970), Chapters 4 and 7.
25. Douglas McGregor, "The Human Side of Enterprise," in Harold Leavitt and Louis Fondy (eds.), *Readings in Managerial Psychology* (Chicago, University of Chicago, 1964), especially pp. 271–73.

26. Maslow, pp. 35–47. McGregor's listing of the five levels in "The Human Side of Enterprise," is quite similar to Maslow's, namely (1) physiological needs, (2) safety needs, (3) social needs, (4) ego needs, and (5) self-fulfill- ment needs—"the capstone as it were on the hierarchy of man's needs." (pp. 271–73).
27. Maslow, p. 99.
28. Charles E. Silberman, *Crisis in Black and White* (New York: Vintage, 1964), p. 335.
29. James A. Wilson, "Citizen Participation in Urban Renewal" in James Q. Wilson (ed.) *Urban Renewal: The Record and the Controversy* (Cambridge: MIT Press, 1966) p. 414.
30. Ibid.
31. Rainwater, pp. 31–2.

Chapter 8
Toward a Theory of Protest

1. James Q. Wilson, "The Strategy of Protest," *Journal of Conflict Resolution,* September, 1961, pp. 291–303.
2. Michael Lipsky, "Protest as a Political Resource," *American Political Science Review,* December, 1968, pp. 1144–58, and Lipsky, *Protest in City Politics,* (Chicago: Rand McNally, 1970).
3. Wilson, p. 292.
4. Lipsky, "Protest as a Political Resource," p. 1146.
5. Ibid., p. 1146n. See also Michael Lipsky and Margaret Levi, "Community Organization as a Political Resource," as delivered at the Sixty-sixty Annual Meeting of the American Political Science Association, September, 1970.
6. I am indebted to Michael Lipsky for having raised this point in a private conversation.
7. Lipsky, *Protest in City Politics,* p. 189.
8. "Welfare," a radio announcement prepared for Governor Sargent by Case and Krone, Inc., New York, New York, October 6, 1970.
9. According to a Survey Research Center study reported in Philip Converse, et al, "Continuity and Change in American Politics," *American Political Science Review* (December, 1969), p. 1105:

The American public seems to have a very low tolerance for unusual or "showy" forms of political dissent. . . . At the most acceptable end of the continuum of "ways for people to show their disagreement with government policies and actions" we asked about "taking part in protest meetings or marches that are permitted by local authorities." Less than 20 per cent of all respondents . . . would approve of such subversive behavior, and more than half would disapprove (the remainder accepted the alternative presented that their reaction "would depend upon the circumstances").

Chapter 9
The Accomplishments of the
Welfare Rights Movement

1. Frances Fox Piven and Richard Cloward, *Regulating the Poor* (New York: Pantheon, 1971), p. 326.

2. These excerpts are from three radio advertisements prepared for Governor Francis Sargent of Massachusetts by Case and Krone, Inc., 4 West 58th Street, New York, New York, entitled "Welfare," "Next Tuesday," and "Name One Thing" (rev.) as produced on October 6, 1970, October 20, 1970, and October 6, 1970 respectively.

3. Discussion with an official of the Department of Health, Education and Welfare on April 24, 1969.

4. One example of this was a three-part series on public welfare on "The CBS Evening News" with Walter Cronkite in May, 1968. One of the three segments was devoted entirely to a discussion of welfare rights and an interview with George Wiley. In other cases the NWRO did not get the coverage it deserved, however. The repetitive nature of much welfare rights activity has sometimes led news editors to downgrade its value as "news" leading to less prominent coverage. The relationship between local group protest activities and the NWRO has been totally ignored by the media on numerous occasions as well.

5. See, for example, the coverage of the NCSW conference in *The New York Times,* May 27, 1969, p. 32.

6. "Welfare Platform Adopted by Massachusetts Democratic Party at State Convention, June 12, 1970," undated mimeographed flyer of the MWRO.

7. A study of the early evolution of the Family Assistance Plan—Franklin D. Raines, "Presidential Policy Development: The Genesis of the Family Assistance Program," unpublished senior thesis, Harvard College, dated April 1, 1971—gives no indication of any impact by the NWRO. Further light is shed upon both the early evolution and the legislative history of the Family Assistance Plan in Daniel P. Moynihan's book *The Politics of a Guaranteed Annual Income* (New York: Random House, 1972).

8. *The New York Times,* April 11, 1971, Section IV, p. 4. The complete list of demands as listed in an advertisement on this page was:

> Set the date for the total withdrawal of all U.S. Armed Forces from Indochina.
>
> Demand a War on Poverty—not on people. Demand a $6500 Guaranteed Annual Income for a family of four.
>
> Free all political prisoners.
>
> End unemployment and inflation.

9. "Memorandum to the Democratic Policy Council from Mrs. Johnie Tillmon, Chairman NWRO and George Wiley Executive Director NWRO," mimeographed by the NWRO and dated May 12, 1971.

10. Helene Levens, "Organizational Affiliation and Powerlessness," *Social Problems*, Summer 1968. Levens reports that 52 per cent of her sample of AFDC mothers belonging to a welfare rights affiliate belonged to no other formal organizations and that 56 per cent of the non-members of welfare rights belonged to no organizations whatsoever.
11. Ibid.
12. Daniel P. Moynihan, *Maximum Feasible Misunderstanding* (New York: Free Press, 1969), p. 107.

Index

Index

About the Author

Lawrence Neil Bailis is Assistant Professor of Political Science at Tufts University and Director of Social Policy Analysis for Contract Research Corporation. He received the B.A. from Cornell University and the M.A. and the Ph.D. in political science from Harvard University, where he was an Honorary Woodrow Wilson Fellow, a National Science Foundation Fellow, and the recipient of the WCBS-TV Fellowship of the Harvard-MIT Joint Center for Urban Studies.